Netbook Basics

Prentice Hall
is an imprint of

PEARSON

Harlow, England • London • New York • Boston • San Francisco • Toronto • Sydney • Singapore • Hong Kong
Tokyo • Seoul • Taipei • New Delhi • Cape Town • Madrid • Mexico City • Amsterdam • Munich • Paris • Milan

PEARSON EDUCATION LIMITED

Edinburgh Gate
Harlow CM20 2JE
Tel: +44 (0) 1279 623623
Fax: +44 (0) 1279 431059
Website: www.pearsoned.co.uk

First published in Great Britain in 2010

ISBN: 978-0-273-73492-5

British Library Cataloguing-in-Publication Data
A catalogue record for this book is available from the British Library

Library of Congress Cataloging-in-Publication Data
Ballew, Joli.
    Netbook basics in simple steps / Joli Ballew.
       p. cm.
    ISBN 978-0-273-73492-5 (pbk.)
  1. Netbook computers.   I. Title.
    QA76.5.B2628 2010
    004.165--dc22
                                2010001305

10 9 8 7 6 5 4 3 2 1
14 13 12 11 10

Designed by pentacorbig, High Wycombe
Typeset in 11/14 pt ITC Stone Sans by 3
Printed and bound by Rotolito Lombarda, Italy

The publisher's policy is to use paper manufactured from sustainable forests.

Netbook Basics

in Simple steps

Joli Ballew

Use your computer with confidence

Get to grips with practical computing tasks with minimal time, fuss and bother.

In Simple Steps guides guarantee immediate results. They tell you everything you need to know on a specific application; from the most essential tasks to master, to every activity you'll want to accomplish, through to solving the most common problems you'll encounter.

Helpful features

To build your confidence and help you to get the most out of your computer, practical hints, tips and shortcuts feature on every page:

 ALERT: Explains and provides practical solutions to the most commonly encountered problems

 HOT TIP: Time and effort saving shortcuts

 SEE ALSO: Points you to other related tasks and information

 DID YOU KNOW? Additional features to explore

WHAT DOES THIS MEAN?
Jargon and technical terms explained in plain English

Practical. Simple. Fast.

Dedication:

For Dad, who continues to show great strength and strong character following Mom's passing; I hope to have Dad's kind heart and pleasant demeanour when I'm his age. He is an inspiration.

Author acknowledgements:

I love writing for Pearson Education, and these In Simple Steps prove it. I've written almost a half dozen of these books and hope to write more in the future. It's wonderful working with Steve Temblett, Laura Blake, and the rest of the gang. It's great when everything just falls together, and we have quite a system going. We know the steps!

I'd also like to thank my family for their continued support, and for sticking by me through the months that I'm overworked, and the various times I'm not. My agent, Neil Salkind, continues to surprise me with his talents, tact, personal support, and connections, and he goes out of his way to keep me busy. Of course I miss my Mom, and am very proud of Dad for trudging through this difficult time with a smile on his face and faith in his heart. Faith is a good thing, and provides hope, security, and sanctuary for those who can find it.

Contents at a glance

Contents

Top 10 Netbook Tips

1 Explore your netbook

8 Use your built-in webcam

9 Work with media

Top 10 Netbook Problems Solved

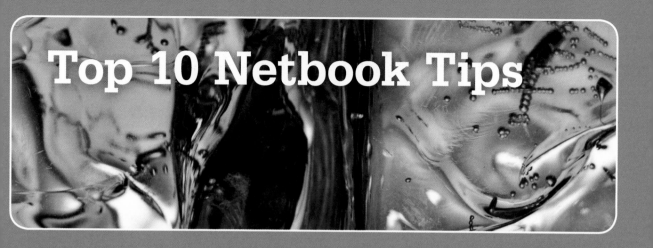

Top 10 Netbook Tips

Tip 1: Search for anything from the Start menu

To locate a program, file, folder, song, picture or anything else stored on your computer, type a little something about it in the Start Search window. In the results, select the appropriate item from the list. Note that when you search using the Start Search window, all kinds of results will appear, including email, applications, documents and pictures.

1 Click Start.

2 In the Start Search window, type Media.

3 Note the results.

4 Click any result to open it. If you want to open Windows Media Player, click it once. Note that it's under Programs.

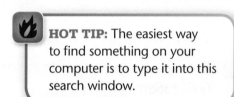

HOT TIP: The easiest way to find something on your computer is to type it into this search window.

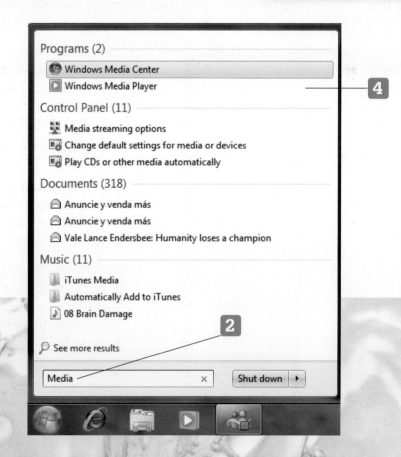

Tip 2: Connect to a free hotspot

You can use your netbook to connect to free Wi-Fi hotspots. Doing so lets you access the Internet without physically connecting to a router or phone line, and without a monthly wireless bill.

 HOT TIP: To find a Wi-Fi hotspot close to you, go to www.maps. google.com and search for Wi-Fi hotspots. You'll find them in various places including airports, hotels, bars, cafes, restaurants and more.

1 Turn on your netbook within range of a wireless network.

2 If you are prompted from the Notification area that wireless networks are available, click Connect to a network (not shown).

3 If you are not prompted to connect to a network, click the network icon in the Notification area.

4 If more than one wireless network is available, locate the one that you want to use and click Connect.

ALERT: Often you'll have to go into the building that offers the wireless connection, or sit right outside, perhaps in a patio area.

ALERT: You will probably want to choose the wireless network with the most green bars.

ALERT: Wi-Fi must be enabled in the Mobility Center or via a switch or keyboard combination to connect to a Wi-Fi network.

5 When prompted, choose Public network.

5

Tip 3: Download and install Windows Live Essentials

Windows 7 does not come with an email program, a photo-editing program or a messaging program. Windows Live Essentials offers all of that and more, and because it's created by Microsoft, you know it's compatible. Did I mention it's free?

1 Open Internet Explorer and go to http://download.live.com/.

2 Look for the Download button and click it. You'll be prompted to click Download once more on the next screen.

3 Click Run and, when prompted, click Yes.

4 When prompted, select the items to download. You can select all of the items or only some of them. (Make sure to at least select Live Mail, Live Messenger and Live Photo Gallery.)

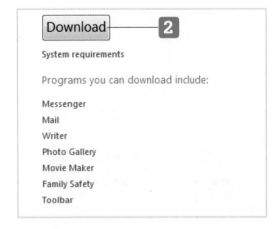

5 Click Install.

6 When prompted to select your settings, make the desired choices. You can't go wrong here; there are no bad options.

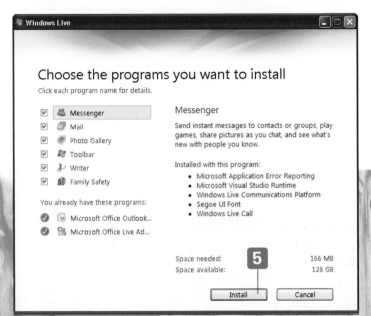

? DID YOU KNOW?

It's OK to select all of these programs if you think you'll use them; they are all free, but don't bog down your netbook with applications you won't use!

Tip 4: Use Office Live Workspace to store important data

You can use Office Live Workspace to store sensitive data you'd rather not leave on your netbook. You can also store data there so you can access it from any computer with Internet access, using your Windows Live ID.

1. Use Internet Explorer and go to http://workspace.officelive.com.

2. Type your Windows Live ID and password and click Sign in.

3. Select your workspace in the left pane.

4. Click Add Documents.

5. Browse to a file to upload, click it, then click Open.

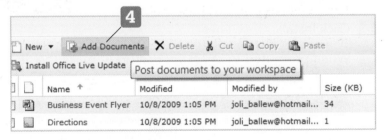

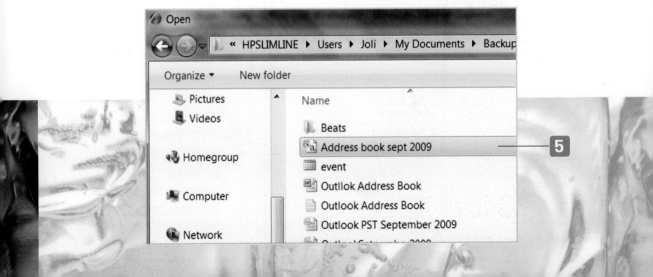

Tip 5: Have a video conversation

Having video conversations using your netbook is some of the most fun you can have. You'll need a webcam and a messaging program, and I prefer Windows Live Messenger. If you have all of that, here's how to do it.

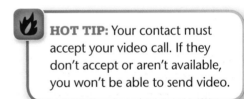

HOT TIP: Your contact must accept your video call. If they don't accept or aren't available, you won't be able to send video.

1 Open Windows Live Messenger and log in.

2 Double-click a contact in your contact list who is online, and who has the required hardware to hold a voice conversation (microphone, speakers and/or headphones).

3 Click Video.

4 Wait while the contact accepts your video call.

5 During the call, the contact will see your webcam. If the recipient has a webcam, you will see theirs.

6 As with a voice call, either person can click Hang up to end the call.

Tip 6: Use Media Player to listen to music

Windows Media Player is an application included with Windows 7. You can watch DVDs and videos here, listen to and manage music, and even listen to radio stations or view pictures.

1 Open Media Player from the taskbar.

2 Click the arrow next to the Library button.

3 Click Music.

4 Click Album. (Note that you can also click Artist or Genre.)

5 Double-click any album to play it.

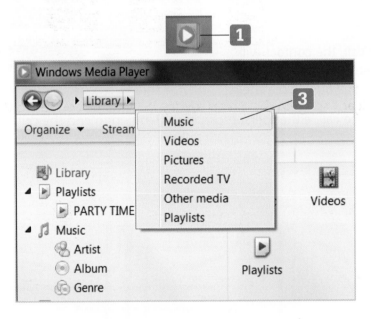

6 Double-click any song on the album to play it. Note the controls at the bottom of the screen.

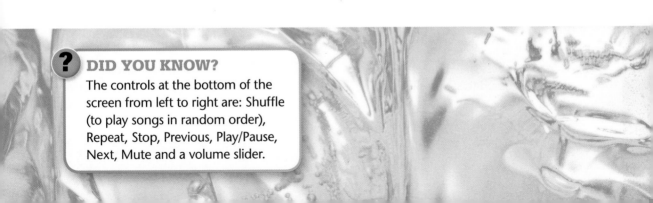

? DID YOU KNOW?

The controls at the bottom of the screen from left to right are: Shuffle (to play songs in random order), Repeat, Stop, Previous, Play/Pause, Next, Mute and a volume slider.

Tip 7: Play a slide show of pictures

If you have pictures on your netbook you want to share with others, show them the pictures in a slide show using Windows Live Photo Gallery.

1 Open Windows Live Photo Gallery.

2 Select any folder that contains pictures.

3 Click the Slide Show button. Wait at least three seconds.

4 To end the show, press the Esc key on the keyboard.

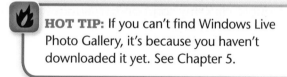

HOT TIP: If you can't find Windows Live Photo Gallery, it's because you haven't downloaded it yet. See Chapter 5.

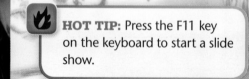

HOT TIP: Press the F11 key on the keyboard to start a slide show.

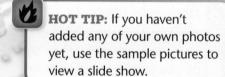

HOT TIP: If you haven't added any of your own photos yet, use the sample pictures to view a slide show.

Tip 8: Connect to a home network

When you connect a new PC running Windows 7 to a wired network or get within range of a wireless one, Windows 7 will find the network and then ask you what kind of network it is. It's a public network if you're in a coffee shop, library or cafe, and it's a private network if it's a network you manage, like one already in your home.

1 Connect physically to a wired network using an Ethernet cable or, if you have wireless hardware installed in your netbook, get within range of a wireless network.

2 Select Home or Work if it's your personal network.

3 You'll be connected automatically.

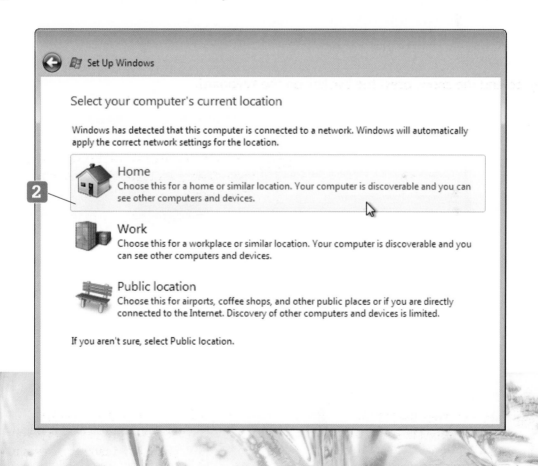

Tip 9: Import pictures from a digital camera or media card

After you've taken pictures with your digital camera, you'll want to move or copy those pictures to your netbook. Once stored on the network's hard drive, you can view, edit, email or print the pictures (among other things). Here's how to import pictures to Windows Live Photo Gallery, part of the free Windows Live Essentials suite of applications.

1 Connect the device or insert the media card into the card reader. If applicable, turn on the camera.

2 When prompted, choose Import Photos and Videos using Windows Live Photo Gallery.

3 Click Import all new items now.

? DID YOU KNOW?
These steps work for importing pictures from a mobile phone too.

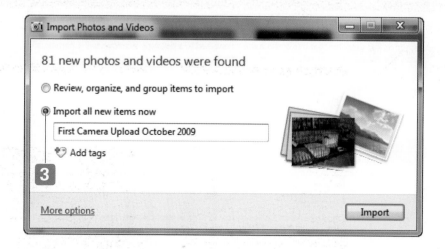

Import Photos and Videos

81 new photos and videos were found

○ Review, organize, and group items to import

◉ Import all new items now

First Camera Upload October 2009

Add tags

3

More options   Import

HOT TIP: If desired, check Erase after importing. This will cause Windows 7 to erase the images from the device after the import is complete.

ALERT: If your device isn't recognised when you plug it in and turn it on, in Windows Live Photo Gallery click File, and click Import from Camera or Scanner.

4 Type a descriptive name for the group of pictures you're importing and click Next.

5 Wait while the import process completes.

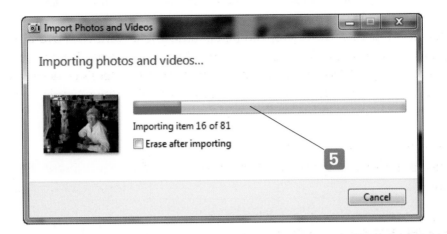

6 View your new photos.

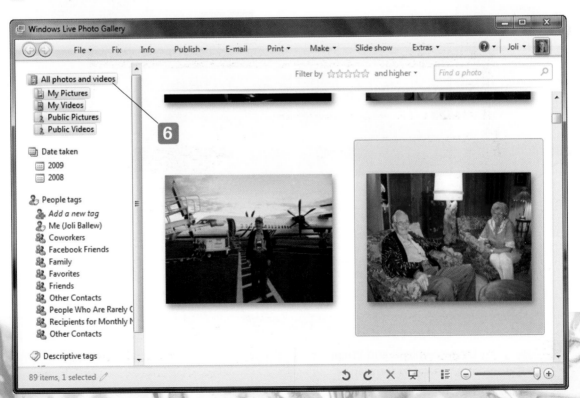

Tip 10: Install software from the Internet

If you can find the program you want to install on the Internet, installation is as simple as downloading the product and following the prompts to install it. This is how you installed Windows Live Essentials in Chapter 5 and device drivers in Chapter 11.

1 Locate the program or driver to install.

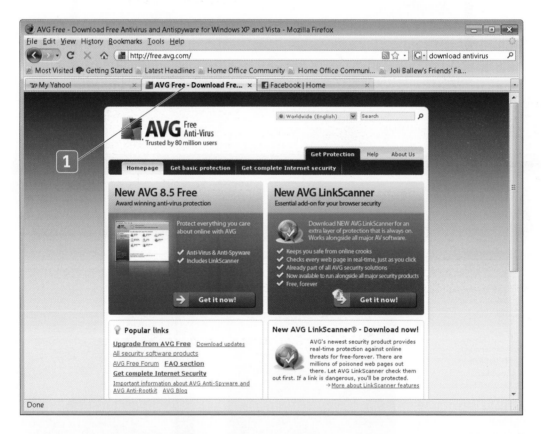

ALERT: Only download and install software from reputable companies with good reviews. Downloaded software can contain malware or viruses.

2 Click the Download or Download Now button.

3 Click Run, and click Run again.

4 Work through the installation wizard.

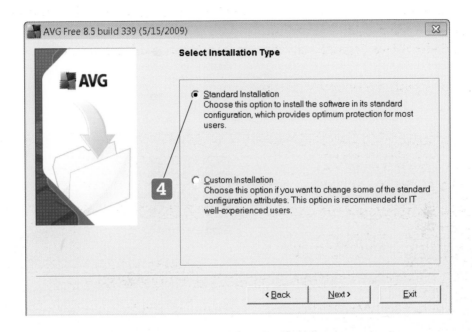

HOT TIP: AVG Free is a free anti-virus program you can download from http://free.avg.com.

1 Explore your netbook

Introduction

A netbook has ports located on the outside of the netbook similar to what you'd expect to see on a desktop PC or a larger laptop; there are Ethernet ports, USB ports and a place to plug in external speakers and headphones, among other things. The keyboard offers the usual array of keys, including Function and Page Up and Page Down keys. Netbooks come with netbook-specific hardware though, including a power button on the keyboard, a bay to hold the battery, and specialised configurable keys you can personalise.

Once you've started your netbook, a process known as 'booting up', you'll probably find it has Windows 7 running on it. This is your netbook's 'operating system', and allows you to operate your netbook, run programs, move the mouse pointer, etc. In this book, I'll assume your new netbook comes with Windows 7, since this is the latest offering from Microsoft.

Plug in the power cable

A power cable is the cable that you will use to connect the netbook to the wall outlet (power outlet). When you connect the power cable to both the netbook and the power outlet, the netbook will use the power from the outlet and charge the battery at the same time. When you unplug the netbook from the power outlet, the netbook will run on stored battery power.

1 Locate the power cord. It may consist of two pieces that need to be connected.

2 Connect the power cord to the back or side of the netbook as noted in the documentation. You may see a symbol similar to the one shown here.

3 Plug the power cord into the wall outlet.

19

HOT TIP: The netbook's battery can only be charged so many times before it has to be replaced. When possible, remove the battery and use a power outlet to extend the battery's life.

HOT TIP: If your new netbook did not come with documentation, visit the manufacturer's website and search for a user's guide.

? DID YOU KNOW?
You can connect and disconnect the power cable at any time, even when the computer is running.

Access and use USB ports

USB ports, or Universal Serial Bus ports, offer a place to connect USB devices. USB devices include mice, external keyboards, mobile phones, digital cameras and other devices, including USB flash drives.

1 Locate a USB cable. The USB cable's length and shape depend on the device, although one end is always small and rectangular.

2 Plug the rectangular end of the USB cable into an empty USB port on your netbook.

3 Connect the other end to the USB device.

4 Often, you'll need to turn on the USB device to have Windows 7 recognise it, but not always.

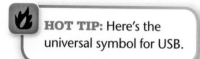

HOT TIP: Here's the universal symbol for USB.

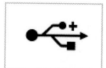

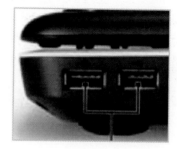

DID YOU KNOW?
You do not generally have to 'turn on' USB storage units, like flash drives.

HOT TIP: FireWire, also called IEEE 1394, is often used to connect digital video cameras, professional audio hardware, and external hard drives to a computer. FireWire ports are larger than USB ports and move data more quickly.

Locate and use Ethernet ports

Ethernet, also called RJ-45, is used to physically connect a netbook to a local network. If you have a cable modem, router or other high-speed Internet device at home, you can use Ethernet to connect to it; and it is worth noting that Ethernet connections are often faster than wireless ones.

1 Locate an Ethernet cable. They are often blue in colour, although they can be grey, white or some other colour.

2 Connect the cable to both the PC and the Ethernet outlet on a router or cable modem.

HOT TIP: An Ethernet cable looks like a telephone cable, except both ends are slightly larger. Here's the universal symbol for Ethernet.

DID YOU KNOW?
When looking for an Ethernet port on your netbook, look for an almost square port. The Ethernet cable will snap in.

Connect external speakers or headphones

If there are any external sound ports, you'll probably see at least two. Most of the time you have access to a microphone-in jack and a headphones/speaker/line-out jack. But there may be others, like a line-in jack.

1 If necessary, plug the device into an electrical outlet (speakers) or insert batteries (portable music players).

2 If necessary, turn on the device.

3 Insert the cables that connect the device to the netbook in the proper port.

4 If prompted, work through any set-up processes.

 DID YOU KNOW?

Line-in jacks bring data into the netbook; line-out jacks port data out to external devices like speakers or headphones.

	Line-in jack
	Microphone-in jack
SPDIF | Headphones/speaker/ line-out jack with S/PDIF support |

WHAT DOES THIS MEAN?

A line-in jack: accepts audio from external devices, like CD players.

A microphone-in jack: accepts input from external microphones.

A headphone or speaker jack: lets you connect your netbook to an external source for output, including but not limited to speakers and headphones.

Locate additional ports

You'll see other ports not mentioned here depending on the make and model of your netbook. You may see ports for a modem, external monitor, FireWire device, serial device, DVI device and media card.

1 Turn the netbook and view all sides of it.

2 View the ports not mentioned here.

3 Here are a few ports you may see on your netbook.

WHAT DOES THIS MEAN?

Kensington lock slot: to connect the netbook to a lock to prevent it from being stolen.

DVI port: DVI stands for Digital Visual Interface, a standard for connecting computers to digital monitors. Because there is no digital to analogue conversion, the images are clearer and of better quality.

S-video: used to connect the netbook to a television or other display that also offers s-video connectivity.

SD card slots or card readers: used to accept digital memory cards found in digital cameras and similar technologies.

ExpressCard: used to insert an ExpressCard where you can expand your netbook's capabilities by offering additional ways to connect devices. ExpressCards are often used to offer wireless capabilities.

AV-in: accepts input from various audio/video devices.

RF-in: accepts input signal from digital TV tuners.

Locate, insert or remove the battery

There are several items that relate to the battery, and they're probably all located on the underside or back of your netbook. Before you turn the netbook upside-down to look at them, make sure you turn off the netbook and unplug it.

1 If the computer is turned off, skip to Step 3.

2 If the computer is turned on, click Start, then click Shut down.

3 Unplug the netbook from the wall outlet and remove the power cable. Set the power cable aside.

4 Close the netbook's lid and carefully turn the netbook upside down and place it on a desk or table.

5 Locate the battery bay and open it, if applicable.

6 Unlatch the battery latch.

7 Remove or install the battery.

8 Lock the battery into place.

9 Secure the latch and close the battery bay door, if applicable.

WHAT DOES THIS MEAN?

Battery bay: this holds the computer's battery. Sometimes you have to use a screwdriver to get inside the battery bay, other times you simply need to slide out the compartment door.

Battery release latch: this latch holds the battery in place, even after the battery bay's door has been opened. You'll need to release this latch to get to the battery.

Battery lock: this locks the battery in position.

Locate the power button and start Windows 7

Before you can use your netbook you have to press the power button on your netbook to start Windows 7.

1 If applicable, open the netbook's lid.

2 Press the Start button to turn on the computer.

? DID YOU KNOW?
Starting a computer is also called 'booting' it.

! ALERT: It takes a minute or so for the computer to start. Be patient!

? DID YOU KNOW?
Most of the time the power button is in the centre of the keyboard, at the very top.

! ALERT: If you ever have trouble starting Windows 7, during the boot-up process hit the F8 key on the keyboard. You can then choose from various start-up options, like 'Safe Mode'.

Activate Windows 7

If this is your first time starting Windows 7, and you're on a new netbook, you'll be prompted to enter some information. Specifically, you'll type your name as you'd like it to appear on your Start menu (capital letters count) and activate Windows 7.

1 Follow the directions on the screen, clicking Next to move from one page of the Activation Wizard to the next.

2 When you have activated Windows 7, wait a few seconds for Windows 7 to initialise.

3 Click the Start button at the bottom of the Windows 7 screen to view your user name.

ALERT: To activate Windows 7 during the initial set-up, you'll have to be connected to the Internet. Alternatively, you can use the phone number provided to activate over the phone.

? DID YOU KNOW?
Activation is mandatory, and if you do not activate Windows within the 30-day time frame, Windows 7 will lose all functionality – except for the activation process.

? DID YOU KNOW?
Usually you can press Enter on the keyboard to activate Next on the screen.

Use the touchpad

When you open your netbook for the first time, you'll probably see a device for moving the mouse, usually a touchpad. You'll use this to move the mouse around the screen.

1 Place your finger on the touchpad and move it around. Notice the mouse moves.

2 If there are buttons, for the most part the left button functions in the same way as the left button on a mouse does.

3 The right button functions the same way as the right button of a mouse does.

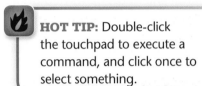

HOT TIP: Double-click the touchpad to execute a command, and click once to select something.

 HOT TIP: Click the right button on the touchpad to open contextual menus to access Copy, Select All and similar commands.

 HOT TIP: Keep your fingers and hands clean when using the touchpad. It has a sensitive surface.

Locate specialised keyboard keys

Most netbook keyboards have more than a few universal keys, and much of the time these keys offer the same things across makes and models. For instance, pressing F1 almost always opens a Help window for the open application, although you may have to press a combination of keys like the Windows key + F1.

1 With the netbook turned on and running, press the F1 key. Often this opens the Getting Started window or Help and Support.

2 Press the Windows key. This often opens the Start menu.

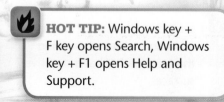
HOT TIP: Windows key + F key opens Search, Windows key + F1 opens Help and Support.

View the Getting Started window

You'll see a Getting Started option on the Start menu. If you hover the mouse over it, you'll see the 'Jump List' that allows you to access a specific task quickly. If you click Getting Started though, the Getting Started window will open.

1 Click Start, and click Getting Started.

2 In the Getting Started window, browse the available features.

3 Click the arrow in the top pane to learn more about the feature selected.

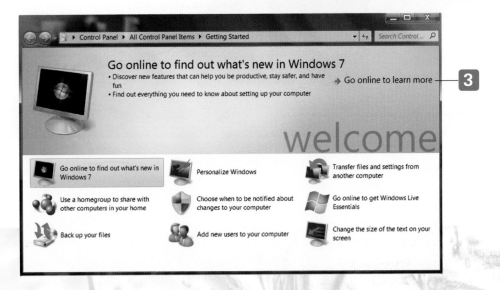

? DID YOU KNOW?

When you click an item in the bottom pane of the Getting Started window, the top pane changes to reflect your choice.

Open Help and Support

Windows 7 offers lots of Help and Support files. You can search Help and Support as you would any website, clicking a link, using the Back button, and even clicking the Home icon to return to the opening Help and Support page.

1 Click Start, and click Help and Support.

2 Click How to get started with your computer.

3 Browse this Help file and explore others.

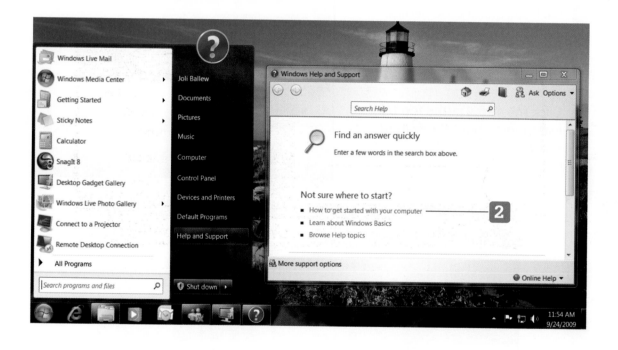

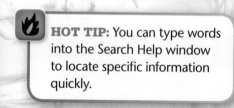

HOT TIP: You can type words into the Search Help window to locate specific information quickly.

Shut down Windows safely

When you're ready to turn off your netbook, it's best to do so using the method detailed here. While most netbooks allow you to close the lid and put the computer to sleep, when you're ready to shut down Windows, you'll need to do it this way.

1 Click Start.

2 Click the arrow to see all of the options.

3 Click Shut down. (Note that you can simply click Shut down without clicking the arrow.)

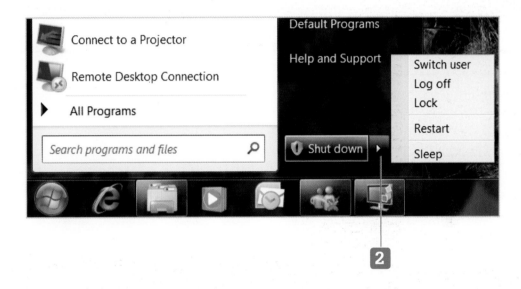

? **DID YOU KNOW?**

Many netbooks now come with a Sleep button on the inside of a netbook. Clicking the Sleep button puts the computer to sleep immediately. If you're taking a break, you might want to try that now instead of completely shutting down the PC.

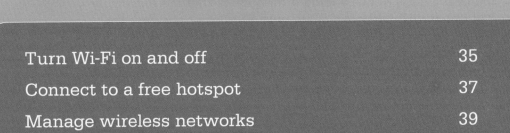

2 Locate and use public Wi-Fi networks

Introduction

One of the best things about having a netbook is that it's extremely easy to get online. All netbooks come with wireless hardware that allows you to connect to Wi-Fi networks easily. One way to get online is to simply get within range of a free Wi-Fi hotspot. Free Wi-Fi hotspots offer public access to the Internet, often benefiting the establishment that offers the access by enticing customers to purchase a cup of coffee or to have a few drinks at the bar.

You may not need hotspots though. If you purchased a wireless plan from an Internet Service Provider, you can get online any time and from anywhere, and you may not see any reason to seek out these free networks. However, you may find that Wi-Fi hotspots offer faster Internet access than your wireless service provider does, for instance. You may also be limited in how much 'bandwidth' you can use each month and want to minimise how much time you spend using your personal wireless connection. Whatever the case, Wi-Fi hotspots are a great way to get online, and should be explored.

Turn Wi-Fi on and off

Before you can connect to a Wi-Fi network, the Wi-Fi feature on your netbook must be enabled. Some netbooks have a switch on the outside of the netbook, while others have a key combination on the keyboard. You should refer to your user's manual to find out exactly how to enable and disable Wi-Fi in this manner.

1 Click Start, and in the Start Search box type Mobility.

2 Click Mobility Center.

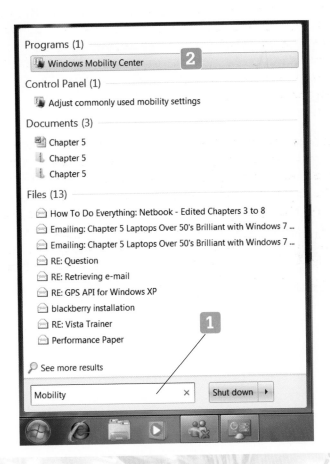

? **DID YOU KNOW?**

You should always turn off Wi-Fi capabilities any time you are told to do so by an airline pilot. With Wi-Fi turned off you can still use your laptop on a plane, once instructed it's OK to use electronic devices.

3 Click Turn wireless off to disable Wi-Fi.

4 Click Turn wireless on to enable it.

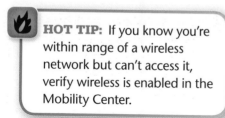 **HOT TIP:** If you know you're within range of a wireless network but can't access it, verify wireless is enabled in the Mobility Center.

ALERT: When wireless is enabled, Windows 7 constantly searches for wireless signals, which uses battery power. You can enable and disable Wi-Fi from the Mobility Center too.

Connect to a free hotspot

You can use your netbook to connect to free Wi-Fi hotspots. Doing so lets you access the Internet without physically connecting to a router or phone line, and without a monthly wireless bill.

1 Turn on your netbook within range of a wireless network.

2 If you are prompted from the Notification area that wireless networks are available, click Connect to a network (not shown).

3 If you are not prompted to connect to a network, click the network icon in the Notification area.

4 If more than one wireless network is available, locate the one that you want to use and click Connect.

 HOT TIP: To find a Wi-Fi hotspot close to you, go to www.maps.google.com and search for Wi-Fi hotspots. You'll find them in various places including airports, hotels, bars, cafes, restaurants and more.

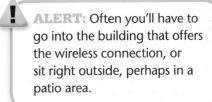 **ALERT:** Often you'll have to go into the building that offers the wireless connection, or sit right outside, perhaps in a patio area.

ALERT: You will probably want to choose the wireless network with the most green bars.

ALERT: Wi-Fi must be enabled in the Mobility Center or via a switch or keyboard combination to connect to a Wi-Fi network.

5 When prompted, choose Public network.

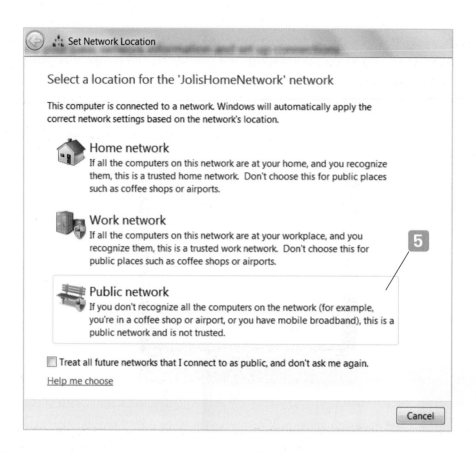

Manage wireless networks

The Network and Sharing Center contains links and access to everything you'll need to manage all of the networks you connect to. You access the Network and Sharing Center by clicking a network icon in the Notification area, among other places. Every wireless network you've ever connected to will be listed in the Manage wireless networks list.

1 Click the network icon in the Notification area. Click Open Network and Sharing Center.

2 In the Network and Sharing Center, note the 'network map'. Here you can see a successful connection to the Internet. (You'd see a red x if there was a problem.)

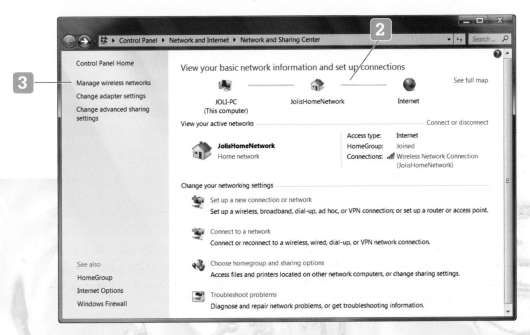

3 Click Manage wireless networks.

4 Select any connection to view its properties or to remove the connection from the list. Note that if more than one wireless network is listed, you'll see additional options. Move the network you connect to most to the top of the list.

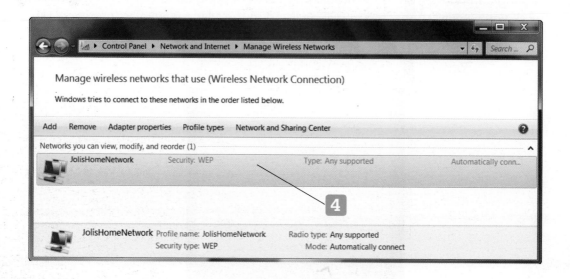

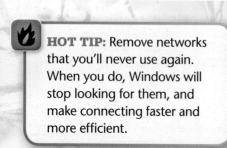

HOT TIP: Remove networks that you'll never use again. When you do, Windows will stop looking for them, and make connecting faster and more efficient.

3 Surf the Internet

Introduction

Having a netbook makes it extremely easy to get online. If you are in range of a free Wi-Fi hotspot you can connect directly to the Internet at no cost at all. The program you'll use to surf the Internet is Internet Explorer. Internet Explorer allows you to open websites, keep multiple webpages open at the same time, configure a home page, mark Favorites and more.

Open a website in Internet Explorer

Windows 7 comes with Internet Explorer, an application you can use to surf the Internet. The first step in web surfing is to open a webpage.

> **! ALERT:** Websites almost always start with http://www.

1 Open Internet Explorer from the taskbar. It's a big, blue E. A website will probably open automatically.

2 To go to a website you want to visit, type the name of the website in the window at the top of the page. This is called the address bar.

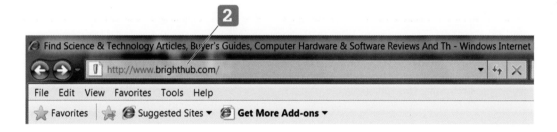

3 Press Enter on the keyboard.

HOT TIP: You can also drag your mouse across an open website name to select it. Do not drag your mouse over the http://www part of the address and you won't have to retype it.

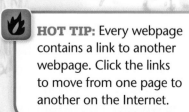

HOT TIP: Every webpage contains a link to another webpage. Click the links to move from one page to another on the Internet.

Open a website in a new tab

You can open more than one website at a time in Internet Explorer. To do this, click the tab that appears to the right of the open webpage. Then, type the name of the website you'd like to visit.

1 Open Internet Explorer.

2 Click an empty tab. Notice a new tab will appear, as shown here.

3 Type the name of the website you'd like to visit in the address bar.

4 Press Enter on the keyboard.

HOT TIP: Type the following: http://www.microsoft.com/uk.

? DID YOU KNOW?
When a website name starts with https://, it means it's secure. When purchasing items online, make sure the payment pages have this prefix.

WHAT DOES THIS MEAN?
The Internet Explorer interface has several distinct parts.
Command bar: used to access icons such as the Home and Print icons.
Tabs: used to access websites when multiple sites are open.
Search window: used to search for anything on the Internet.

Set a home page

You can select a single webpage or multiple webpages to be displayed each time you open Internet Explorer. In fact, there are three options for configuring home pages:

- Use this webpage as your only home page – select this option if you only want one page to serve as your home page.
- Add this webpage to your home page tabs – select this option if you want this page to be one of several home pages.
- Use the current tab set as your home page – select this option if you've opened multiple tabs and you want all of them to be home pages.

1 Use the address bar to locate a webpage you want to use as your home page.

2 Click the arrow next to the Home icon.

3 Click Add or Change Home Page.

4 Make a selection using the information provided regarding each option. If you've never set a home page before, you'll need to select Use this webpage as your only home page.

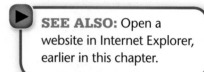
SEE ALSO: Open a website in Internet Explorer, earlier in this chapter.

5 Click Yes.

6 Repeat these steps as desired.

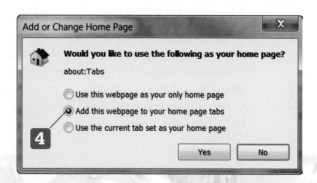

Add or Change Home Page

Would you like to use the following as your home page?

about:Tabs

○ Use this webpage as your only home page
◉ Add this webpage to your home page tabs
○ Use the current tab set as your home page

4

Yes   No

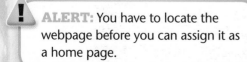
ALERT: You have to locate the webpage before you can assign it as a home page.

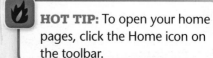
HOT TIP: To open your home pages, click the Home icon on the toolbar.

Mark a Favorite

Favorites are websites you save links to for accessing more easily at a later time. They differ from home pages because by default, they do not open when you start Internet Explorer. The Favorites you save appear in the Favorites Center and on the Favorites bar. You may see some Favorites listed that you did not create, including Microsoft Websites and MSN Websites. Every time you save a Favorite, it will appear in both the Favorites Center and the Favorites bar.

1 Go to the webpage you want to configure as a Favorite.

2 Click the Add to Favorites icon.

3 Note the new icon for the Favorite on the Favorites bar.

4 Click the Favorites icon. The Favorites Center opens.

5 Click the folders to view the Favorites listed in them.

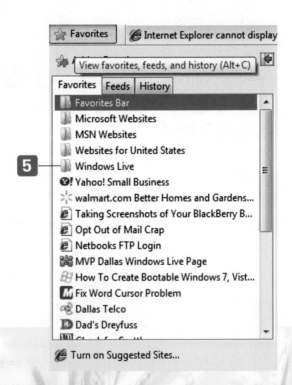

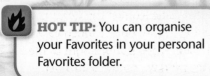

HOT TIP: You can organise your Favorites in your personal Favorites folder.

Change the zoom level of a webpage

If you have trouble reading what's on a webpage because the text is too small, use the Page Zoom feature. Page Zoom works by preserving the fundamental design of the webpage you're viewing. This means that Page Zoom intelligently zooms in on the entire page, which maintains the page's integrity, layout and look.

1 Open Internet Explorer and browse to a webpage.

2 Click the arrow located at the bottom right of Internet Explorer to show the Zoom options.

3 Click 150%.

4 Notice how the webpage text and images increase. Use the scroll bars to navigate the page.

? DID YOU KNOW?

The term browse is used to describe both locating a file on your hard drive and locating something on the Internet.

? DID YOU KNOW?

The Page Zoom options are located under the Page icon on the Command bar, under Zoom, but it's much easier to use the link at the bottom right of the browser window, on the Status bar.

Print a webpage

To print a webpage, simply click the Print icon on the Command bar.

1 Open Internet Explorer and browse to a webpage.

2 Click the Print icon to print the page with no further input. To view print options, click the arrow next to the Print icon, as shown here.

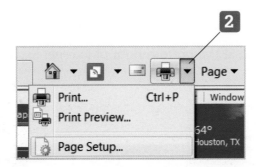

WHAT DOES THIS MEAN?

There are three menu options under the Print icon:

Print: clicking Print opens the Print dialogue box where you can configure the page range, select a printer, change page orientation, change print order and choose a paper type. Additional options include print quality, output bins and more. Of course, the choices offered depend on what your printer offers. If your printer can only print at 300 × 300 dots per inch, you can't configure it to print at a higher quality.

Print Preview: clicking Print Preview opens a window where you can see before you print what the print-out will actually look like. You can switch between portrait and landscape views, access the Page Setup dialog box, and more.

Page Setup: clicking Page Setup opens the Page Setup dialogue box. Here you can select a paper size, source and create headers and footers. You can also change orientation and margins, all of which is dependent on what features your printer supports.

Clear history

If you don't want people to be able to snoop around on your computer and find out what sites you've been visiting you'll need to delete your 'browsing history'. Deleting your browsing history lets you remove the information stored on your computer related to your Internet activities.

1 Open Internet Explorer.

2 Click Safety.

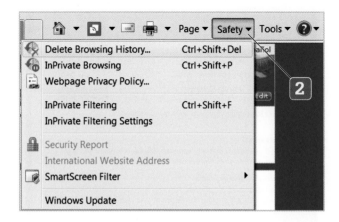

WHAT DOES THIS MEAN?

Temporary Internet Files: these are files that have been downloaded and saved in your Temporary Internet Files folder. A snooper could go through these files to see what you've been doing online.

Cookies: these are small text files that include data that identifies your preferences when you visit particular websites. Cookies are what allow you to visit, say, www.amazon.co.uk and be greeted with Hello <your name>, We have recommendations for you! Cookies help a site offer you a personalised web experience.

History: this is the list of websites you've visited and web addresses you've typed. Anyone can look at your History list to see where you've been.

Form data: this is information that's been saved using the Internet Explorer's autocomplete form data functionality. If you don't want forms to be filled out automatically by you or someone else who has access to your PC and user account, delete this.

Passwords: these are passwords that were saved using Internet Explorer autocomplete password prompts.

InPrivate Blocking data: these are data that were saved by InPrivate Blocking to detect where websites may be automatically sharing details about your visit.

3 Click Delete Browsing History.

4 To delete any or all of the listed items, click the Delete button.

5 Click Close when finished.

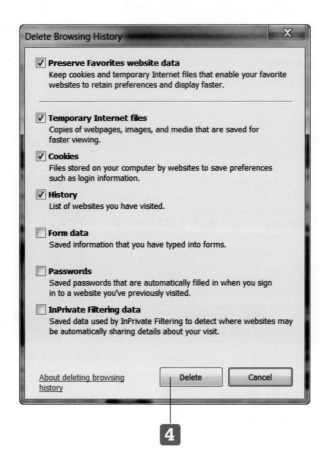

4

Stay safe online

There's a chapter in this book on security, Chapter 13. In it, you'll learn how to use Windows Firewall, Windows Defender and other Security Center features. However, much of staying secure when online and surfing the Internet has more to do with common sense. When you're online, make sure you follow the guidelines listed next.

1 If you are connecting to a public network, make sure you select Public when prompted by Windows 7.

2 Always keep your netbook secure with anti-virus software.

3 Limit the amount of confidential information you store on the Internet.

4 When making credit card purchases or travel reservations, always make sure the website address starts with https://.

5 Always sign out (logout) of any secure website you enter.

? DID YOU KNOW?
When you connect to a network you know, like a network in your home, you select Home (or Work).

! ALERT: You have to purchase and install your own anti-virus software; it does not come with Windows 7.

WHAT DOES THIS MEAN?

Domain name: for our use here, a domain name is synonymous with a website name.

Favorite: a webpage that you've chosen to maintain a shortcut for in the Favorites Center.

Home page: the webpage that opens when you open Internet Explorer. You can set the home page and configure additional pages to open as well.

Link: a shortcut to a webpage. Links are often offered in an email, document or webpage to allow you to access a site without having to actually type in its name. In almost all instances, links are underlined and in a different colour from the rest of the type on the page they are configured on.

Load: a webpage must 'load' before you can access it. Some pages load instantly, while others take a few seconds.

Navigate: the process of moving from one webpage to another or viewing items on a single webpage. Often the term is used as follows: 'Click the link to navigate to the new web page'.

Search: a term used when you type a word or group of words into a Search window. Searching for data produces results.

Scroll Up and Scroll Down: a process of using the scroll bars on a webpage or the arrow keys on a keyboard to move up and down the pages of a website.

Website: a group of webpages that contain related information. Microsoft's website contains information about Microsoft products, for instance.

URL: stands for Uniform Resource Locator, and is the information you type to access a website, like http://www.microsoft.com.

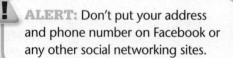

ALERT: Don't put your address and phone number on Facebook or any other social networking sites.

HOT TIP: The s after http lets you know it's a secure site.

4 Obtain always-on Internet

Introduction

You already know that you can get online for free at no-cost Wi-Fi hotspots. However, if you want to get online from anywhere and at any time you'll need to sign on with an Internet Service Provider (ISP) and pay a monthly fee. There are lots of Internet providers and ways to connect. There's dial-up, broadband and satellite, for instance. Only one of these options is appropriate for a netbook though: you need a wireless connection from a satellite Internet provider.

Select an ISP

There are lots of companies that offer wireless access to the Internet. You should shop around before committing to any service, because usually, you have to sign a contract for a year or more, and you want to make sure you're getting the service you want. Ask friends and relatives what they use and for their opinion. If you have a mobile phone you pay for monthly, ask them too. You may get a discount on a wireless subscription if you bundle it with your mobile phone bill.

When shopping for an ISP, ask the following questions:

1 Is there a limit on how much bandwidth I can use each month? Is there a limit on how many hours I can be online? (The answer should be no.)

2 Will I get a free email address with my service? (The answer can be yes or no; you can use your Windows Live email address if not.)

3 How much is the service per month? How much will taxes and fees add to that? (Look for an honest answer in a price range you can afford.)

4 Are there any set-up costs? (The answer should be no.)

5 Am I required to purchase additional hardware? (The best answer is no, but many companies require you to purchase a USB Wi-Fi adapter, often called a 'Wi-Fi stick', and plug it into your netbook for access.)

6 Is there a specific amount of time I can be online before I'm automatically disconnected (when the connection times out)? (The answer should be no.)

7 Is there a 30-day return policy or grace period, in case the connection is not as good or strong as I had hoped? (The answer should be yes.)

Obtain the proper settings

Once you've decided on an ISP, you'll need to call them to set up the subscription. There are some important things to ask the representative, and you must write these things down and keep them in a safe place. Note that not all of these items are applicable to all Internet subscriptions. In some instances you won't need any of these things.

1 User name – used to log on to the Internet.

2 Account name (may be the same as user name) – used to log onto the Internet and/or to set up your email account.

3 Password – used to secure your Internet connection.

4 Email address – used to send and receive email. If you already have an email address and don't want to set up another, you can skip this and Steps 5 and 6.

5 Incoming POP3 server name – used to set up your email account in Windows Mail.

6 Outgoing SMTP server name – used to set up your email account in Windows Mail.

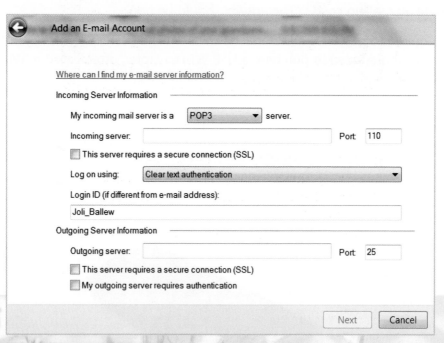

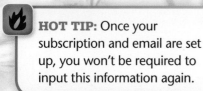

HOT TIP: Once your subscription and email are set up, you won't be required to input this information again.

Make the connection

Before you can connect to the Internet, you need to install any hardware you received. This may mean inserting a USB satellite adapter. Generally, the first time the USB stick is inserted, the installation program runs automatically.

1 Insert the USB Wi-Fi adapter and work through the installation process, if applicable.

2 If no installation is required, follow the instructions provided by your ISP.

3 You should be able to click a Connect button similar to this one, to connect easily to the Internet.

! **ALERT:** Don't be alarmed if you aren't prompted for anything, not even a user name. Many Internet subscriptions for netbooks don't require it.

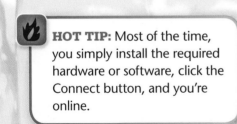

HOT TIP: Most of the time, you simply install the required hardware or software, click the Connect button, and you're online.

Select a network type

The first time you connect to any network you'll be prompted to select a network type.

Here's how to choose.

- **Home:** Choose this if the network is your home network or a network you trust (like a network at a friend's house). This connection type lets your computer *discover* other PCs, printers and devices on the network, and they can see you.
- **Work:** Choose this if you are connecting to a network at work. The settings for Work and Home are the same, only the titles differ so you can tell them apart easily.
- **Public Network Location:** Choose this if the network you want to connect to is open to anyone within range of it, like networks in coffee shops, airports and libraries. Windows 7 figures if you choose Public, you only want to connect to the Internet and nothing else. It closes down *discoverability*, so that even your shared data is safe.

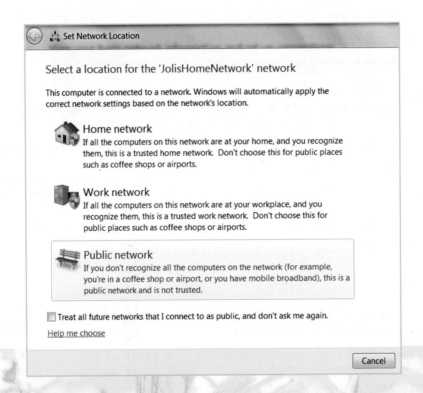

Use the New Connection Wizard

You may be told you have to work through the New Connection Wizard to set up your wireless connection. This is unlikely, but it's included here just in case. You can follow these steps to connect to a local wireless network later, if you like.

1 Click Start, and in the Start Search window type Network and Sharing.

2 In the results, click Network and Sharing Center.

3 Click Set up a new connection or network.

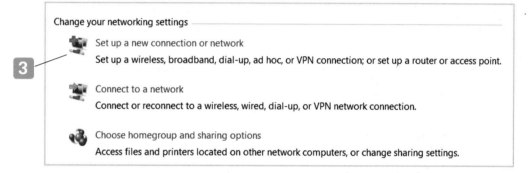

3 Change your networking settings

Set up a new connection or network
Set up a wireless, broadband, dial-up, ad hoc, or VPN connection; or set up a router or access point.

Connect to a network
Connect or reconnect to a wireless, wired, dial-up, or VPN network connection.

Choose homegroup and sharing options
Access files and printers located on other network computers, or change sharing settings.

4 Click Connect to the Internet – Set up a wireless, broadband or dial-up connection to the Internet. Click Next.

5 Select Wireless.

6 If prompted, fill in the required information and click Create. Otherwise, select the wireless connection from the resulting list of available networks. Note – you may already be connected!

7 If you are not connected to a wireless network, select the network and click Connect.

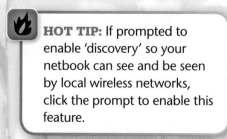

HOT TIP: If prompted to enable 'discovery' so your netbook can see and be seen by local wireless networks, click the prompt to enable this feature.

Diagnose connection problems

If you are having trouble connecting to the Internet through a public or private network, you can diagnose Internet problems using the Network and Sharing Center.

1 Open the Network and Sharing Center.

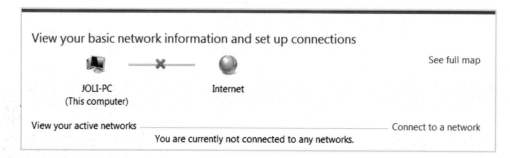

View your basic network information and set up connections

See full map

JOLI-PC
(This computer)

Internet

View your active networks ─────────────────────────── Connect to a network
You are currently not connected to any networks.

2 To diagnose a nonworking Internet connection, click the red X.

3 Click the first solution to resolve the connectivity problem.

4 Often, the problem is resolved. If it is not, move to the next step and the next until it is.

5 Click the X in the top right corner of the Network and Sharing window to close it.

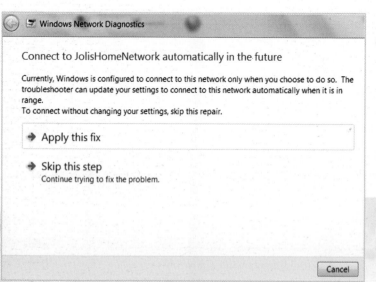

Windows Network Diagnostics

Connect to JolisHomeNetwork automatically in the future

Currently, Windows is configured to connect to this network only when you choose to do so. The troubleshooter can update your settings to connect to this network automatically when it is in range.
To connect without changing your settings, skip this repair.

➡ Apply this fix

➡ Skip this step
Continue trying to fix the problem.

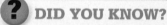

Cancel

ALERT: If you are connected to the Internet, you will see a green line between your computer and the Internet. If you are not connected you will see a red X.

? DID YOU KNOW?
There are additional troubleshooting tips in the Help and Support pages. Click Start, then click Help and Support.

5 Get Windows Live Essentials

Introduction

Windows 7 doesn't come with an email program, a messaging program, or a photo-editing program. Windows Vista did, and Windows XP did, but not Windows 7. You'll need to choose the programs you want to replace these, and we suggest Windows Live Essentials. Once you've installed Live Essentials, obtained an ID, and signed in, you'll have access to a personalised webpage you can customise.

Windows Live Essentials contains all of the programs you'll need to manage email, instant message with contacts, edit photos and even create and edit your own movies. You can choose to install additional applications from the suite too, including the Internet Explorer toolbar that connects all of this together seamlessly.

Download and install Windows Live Essentials

If you've never downloaded and/or installed a program before, you may be a little nervous about doing so. Don't worry, it's really easy, and Microsoft has set it up so that the process requires very little input from you. There are only a few steps: go to the website, click the Download link, and wait for the download and installation process to complete.

1 Open Internet Explorer and go to http://download.live.com/.

2 Look for the Download button and click it. You'll be prompted to click Download once more on the next screen.

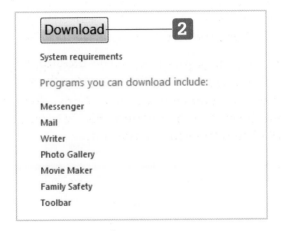

3 Click Run, and when prompted, click Yes.

4 When prompted, select the items to download. You can select all of the items or only some of them. (Make sure to at least select Live Mail and Live Photo Gallery.)

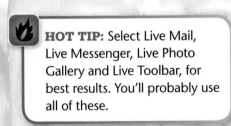

HOT TIP: Select Live Mail, Live Messenger, Live Photo Gallery and Live Toolbar, for best results. You'll probably use all of these.

5 Click Install.

6 When prompted to select your settings, make the desired choices. You can't go wrong here; there are no bad options.

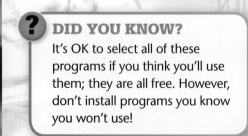

DID YOU KNOW?

It's OK to select all of these programs if you think you'll use them; they are all free. However, don't install programs you know you won't use!

Get a Windows Live ID

When you use 'Live' services, like Windows Live Mail, Windows Live Photo Gallery and others, you have to log into them using a Windows Live account. This account is free, and you can use it to sign into Live-related websites on the Internet. A Windows Live account is an email address and password you use to log onto your Live programs on the Internet.

1 If you do not already have a Windows Live account, click Sign up after the installation of Live Mail completes. (You can also go to http://signup.live.com.)

2 Fill out the required information and click I accept when finished.

 DID YOU KNOW?
You can use your Windows Live email account as a regular email address, or simply use it to log into Live services on the Internet.

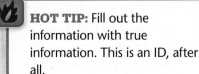 **HOT TIP:** Fill out the information with true information. This is an ID, after all.

Sign in

Once you've obtained your Windows Live ID, you can log into Live services like Windows Live Mail and Windows Live Photo Gallery. But what's even better than that is that you now have a personalised webpage on the Internet.

1 Open Internet Explorer and navigate to http://login.live.com.

2 Type your new Live ID and password and click Sign in.

3 Click Home.

Personalise your Windows Live Home page

Along with the free Live programs, you'll also get a personalised webpage. You can configure the options on the page to suit your needs. For instance, if you input your zip code you'll get personalised weather information.

1 Log into your new Windows Live Home page, as detailed in the previous section.

2 Click Options, and click Customize this page.

3 Input the desired data, including your postcode.

4 Decide how the page should look.

5 Click Save.

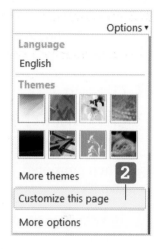

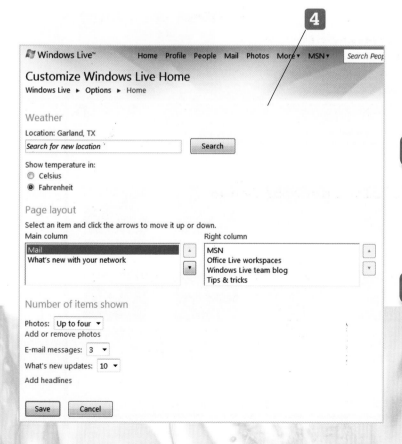

HOT TIP: Click Photos at the top of the page to create an album and upload your favourite photos!

HOT TIP: If you want to use your Live email address, you can get your email right from your Home page. You can also add contacts, share photos and view private messages from people you know.

Open Windows Live Photo Gallery

In the next chapter you'll learn all about Windows Live Mail. For now though, open Windows Live Photo Gallery to see what you've downloaded. Live Photo Gallery will help you manage, edit and store your digital photos.

1 Click Start, click All Programs.

2 Click Windows Live, and then click Windows Live Photo Gallery.

3 When prompted, log in with your new Windows Live ID.

4 To view the sample pictures that come with Windows 7, click Sample Pictures in the left pane.

5 Try clicking any picture, and you will notice how the menu bar changes. One option is Fix, which allows you to edit pictures easily.

6 Windows Live Mail

Introduction

Previous versions of Windows operating systems, like Windows XP and Windows Vista, came with an email program already built in. That's not the case with Windows 7. However, Microsoft does offer Windows Live Mail, which you can download and install for free on your Windows 7 PC. Windows Live Mail lets you access your email from any PC that has Internet access, not just the PC in your home or office.

What is Windows Live Mail?

Windows Live Mail is the only thing you need to view, send and receive email, manage your contacts and manage sent, saved and incoming email. Within Windows Live Mail you can also print email, create folders for storing email you want to keep, manage unwanted email, open attachments, send pictures inside an email and more.

To use Windows Live Mail you'll need to complete some of the tasks already outlined in this book, including downloading and installing Live Mail (Chapter 5), and having access to a wireless hotspot (Chapter 2) or having some form of personal Internet access like an always-on subscription (Chapter 4). You'll also need to gather any personalised email information given to you from your ISP, also outlined in Chapter 4, like server names, your email address and password.

Set up a Windows Live email account

The first time you open Windows Live Mail you'll be prompted to input the required information regarding your email address and email servers. That's because Windows Live Mail is a program for sending and receiving email, and you can't do that without inputting the proper information. The easiest email account to set up is your new Windows Live account. That's what you'll do here.

1 Open Windows Live Mail.

2 Click Add an E-mail Account.

3 Type your Windows Live email address, password and display name.

4 If desired, leave Remember Password ticked. Click Next.

5 Click Finish, and if prompted, click Download Now to retrieve your email. (Don't check Manually configure server settings for e-mail account.)

? DID YOU KNOW?

Your email address often takes this form: *yourname@Live.com*. Your display name can be anything you like.

? DID YOU KNOW?

Your display name is the name that will appear in the From field when you compose an email, and in the sender's inbox (under From in their email list) when people receive email from you.

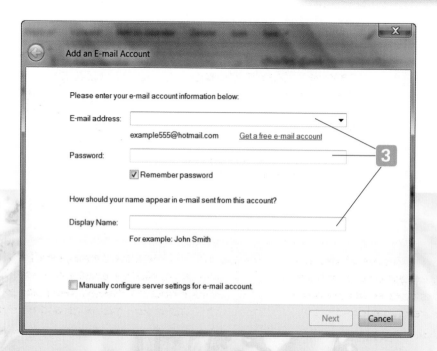

Set up a third-party email account

When you set up a Windows Live email account, Windows Live knows what settings to use and configure in the background. If you want to set up a third-party email account, you have to enter the settings manually. You get the information you need from your ISP.

1 Open Mail, and click Add an E-mail Account as detailed in the previous section.

2 Input your email address, password and display name.

3 When prompted, fill in the information for your incoming and outgoing mail servers. Click Next.

4 Click Next. Click Finish.

DID YOU KNOW?
Popular ISPs include BT, TalkTalk, AOL, Virgin Media, Tiscali and Sky Broadband amongst others.

ALERT: You must input exactly what your ISP tells you to input! When in doubt, call the ISP or check their website for the proper settings.

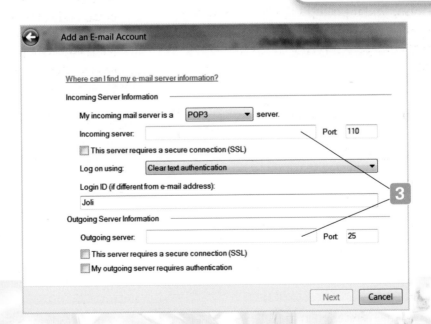

ALERT: If your ISP told you your outgoing server requires authentication, tick the box. If you aren't sure, don't tick it.

ALERT: To resolve errors, click Tools, click Accounts, click the email account to change and click Properties. You can then make changes to the mail servers, passwords and other settings.

View an email

Windows Live Mail checks for email automatically when you first open the program and every 30 minutes thereafter. If you want to check for email manually, you can click the Sync button any time you want. When you receive mail, there are two ways to read it. You can click the message once and read it in the Mail window, or double-click it to open it in its own window. I think it's best to simply click the email once – that way you don't have multiple open windows to deal with.

1 Click the Sync button.

2 Click the email once.

3 View the contents of the email.

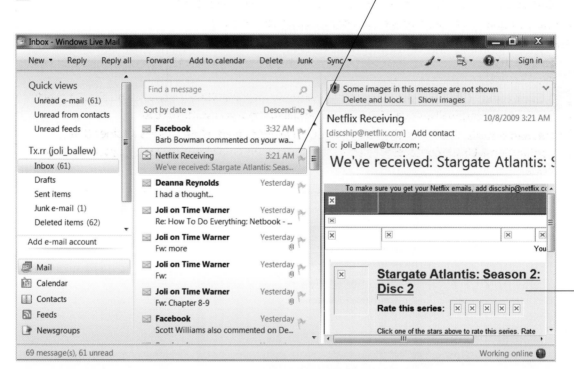

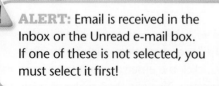 **ALERT:** Email is received in the Inbox or the Unread e-mail box. If one of these is not selected, you must select it first!

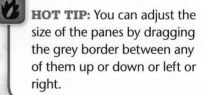 **HOT TIP:** You can adjust the size of the panes by dragging the grey border between any of them up or down or left or right.

WHAT DOES THIS MEAN?

Inbox: this folder holds mail you've received.

Outbox: this folder holds mail you've written but have not yet sent.

Sent items: this folder stores copies of messages you've sent.

Deleted items: this folder holds mail you've deleted.

Drafts: this folder holds messages you've started and saved, but not completed. Click File and click Save to put an email in progress here.

Junk e-mail: this folder holds email that Windows Live Mail thinks is spam. You should check this folder occasionally, since Mail may put email in there you want to read.

Unread e-mail: this folder shows email you have yet to read. Note there is a folder that contains email from contacts too. The latter only shows email from contacts in your address book.

Change how often Mail checks for email

You may want Mail to check for email more or less often than every 30 minutes. It's easy to make the change.

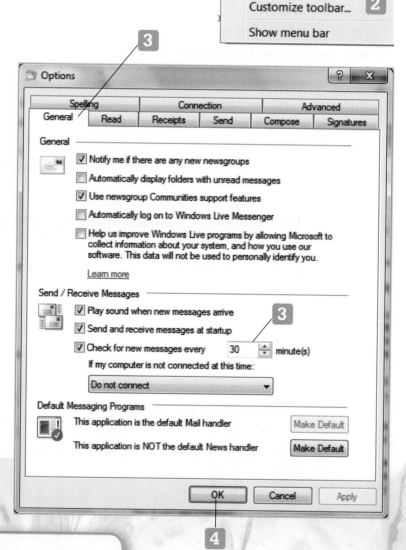

1 Click the Menu icon.

2 Click Options.

3 On the General tab, under Send/Receive Messages, change the number of minutes from 30 to something else.

4 Click OK.

DID YOU KNOW?

You can change other settings in Mail from the other tabs in the Options dialogue box.

View an attachment

An attachment is a file that you can send with an email such as a picture, document, video clip or something similar. If an email you receive contains an attachment, you'll see a paperclip. To open the attachment, click the attachment's name.

ALERT: Hackers send attachments that look like they are from legitimate companies, banks and online services. Do not open these. Companies rarely send email attachments.

1 Locate the paperclip icon in the Message pane. Note the name of the attachment(s).

2 If the attachment is something you are expecting and you know the sender, double-click the attachment name.

3 If prompted, click Open.

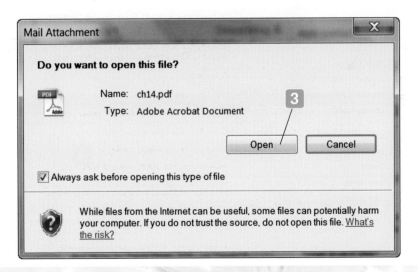

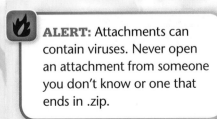
ALERT: Attachments can contain viruses. Never open an attachment from someone you don't know or one that ends in .zip.

Recover email from the Junk e-mail folder

Windows Live Mail has a junk email filter and anything it thinks is spam gets sent there. (Spam is another word for junk email.) Unfortunately, sometimes email gets sent to the Junk e-mail folder that is actually legitimate email. Therefore, once a week or so you should look in this folder to see if any email you want to keep is in there.

1 Click the Junk e-mail folder once.

2 Use the scroll bars if necessary to browse through the email in the folder.

3 If you see an email that is legitimate, click it once.

4 Click Not junk.

5 After reviewing the files, click Inbox.

 HOT TIP: When you tell Mail that a certain email is 'not junk', it remembers and should not flag email from this sender as spam again.

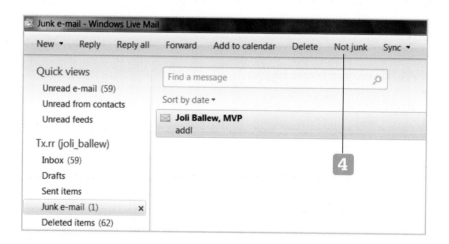

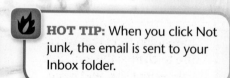 **HOT TIP:** When you click Not junk, the email is sent to your Inbox folder.

! ALERT: Mail requires routine maintenance including deleting email from the Junk e-mail folder, among others. You'll learn how to delete items in a folder later in this chapter.

Reply to an email

When someone sends you an email, you may need to send a reply back to them. You do that by selecting the email and then clicking the Reply button.

1 Select the email you want to reply to in the Message pane.

2 Click Reply.

3 Type the message in the body pane.

4 Click Send.

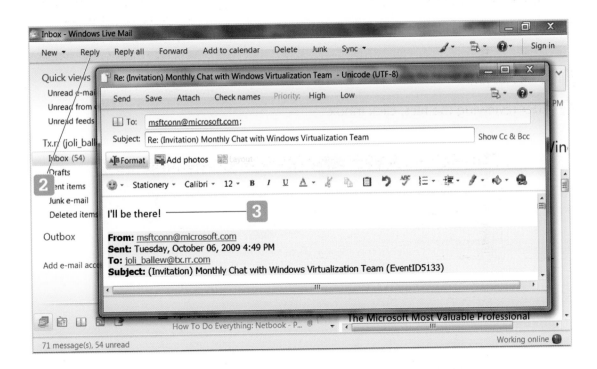

ALERT: If the email you are replying to was sent to you along with additional people, clicking Reply will send a reply to the person who composed the message. Clicking Reply all will send the reply to everyone who received the email.

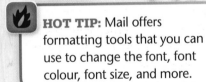 **HOT TIP:** Mail offers formatting tools that you can use to change the font, font colour, font size, and more.

Forward an email

When someone sends you an email that you want to share with others, you forward the email. You do that by selecting the email and then clicking the Forward button.

1 Select the email you want to forward in the Message pane.

2 Click Forward.

3 Complete the email by adding an address to the To line and writing something in the message body.

4 Click Send.

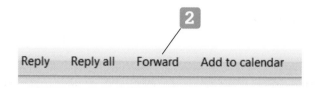

DID YOU KNOW?
People often forward funny jokes.

 HOT TIP: To send a single email to multiple recipients, separate each email address by a semicolon.

DID YOU KNOW?
Forwarded email contains FW: in the subject line by default.

Compose and send a new email

You compose an email message by clicking New on the toolbar. You input who the email should be sent to, the subject, and then you type the message.

81

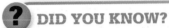

DID YOU KNOW?
When working with email, make sure Mail is selected in the bottom left corner of the Live Mail window. Other options include Calendar, Contacts, Feeds and Newsgroups.

1 Click New.

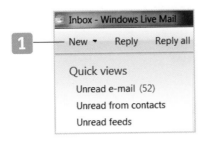

2 Type the recipient's name or email address in the To line. If you want to add additional names, separate each email address by a semicolon.

3 Click Check names. This verifies the email address and puts a line under the address in the To line.

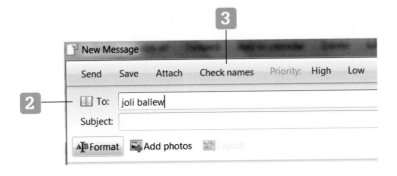

4 Type a subject in the Subject field.

HOT TIP: Click the address book icon next to the To line to add email addresses from your address book.

HOT TIP: Make sure the subject adequately describes the body of your email. Your recipients should be able to review the subject line later and be able to recall what the email was regarding.

5 Type the message in the body pane.

6 Click Send.

6

WHAT DOES THIS MEAN?
Cc: stands for carbon copy.
Bcc: stands for blind carbon copy and is a secret copy.

Attach a picture to an email using Attach

Although email that contains only a message serves its purpose quite a bit of the time, often you'll want to send a photograph, a short video, a sound recording, document or other data. When you want to add something to your message other than text, it's called adding an attachment. There are many ways to attach something to an email. One way is to use the Attach command.

1 Click New to create a new mail message.

2 Click Attach.

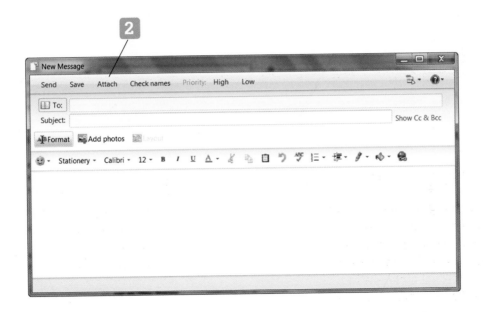

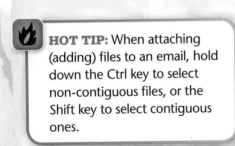

HOT TIP: When attaching (adding) files to an email, hold down the Ctrl key to select non-contiguous files, or the Shift key to select contiguous ones.

3 Locate the file to attach.

4 Double-click the file to attach.

Attach a picture to an email using a right-click

You can create an email that contains an attachment by right-clicking the file you want to attach. This method attaches the files to a new email, which is fine if you want to create a new email. The only problem with this is that it doesn't work if you'd rather send forwards or replies. However, this method has a feature other methods don't. With this method, you can resize any images you've selected before sending them.

1 Locate the file you'd like to attach and right-click it.

2 Point to Send To.

3 Click Mail Recipient.

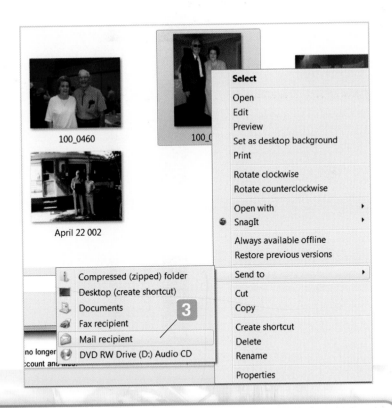

? **DID YOU KNOW?**

You can email from within applications, such as Microsoft Word or Excel. Generally, you'll find the desired option under the File menu, as a submenu of Send or from the Office button in the top left corner of many newer Microsoft Office applications.

4 If the item you're attaching is a picture, choose the picture size. Click Attach.

5 Complete the email and click Send.

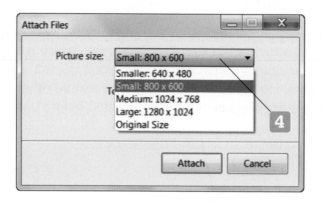

Insert a picture directly into the body of the email

Windows Live Mail offers a new feature where you can add images to the body of the email and edit them before sending. You can even put 'frames' around them, have Windows 'autocorrect' colour and brightness, and add more photos easily.

1 Click New to open a new email.

2 Click Add photos.

3 Browse to the photo(s) to add, and double-click them to add them.

4 Click any photo to add text, add a frame or rotate, among other options.

5 Complete the email, and when ready, click Send.

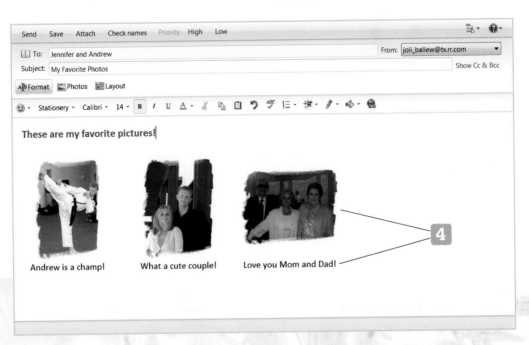

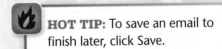
HOT TIP: To save an email to finish later, click Save.

Add a contact

A contact is a data file that holds the information you keep about a person. The contact information looks like a 'contact card', and the information can include a picture, email address, mailing address, first and last name and similar data. You obtain contacts from various sources: people you email, people you instant message with Windows Live Messenger, and more.

1 From Windows Live Mail, click Contacts.

2 Click New.

3 Type all of the information you desire to add. Be sure to add information to each tab.

4 Click Add contact (not shown).

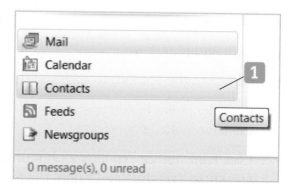

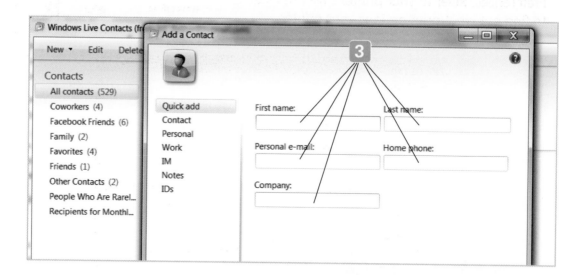

HOT TIP: Your contacts are stored in your Contacts folder inside your personal folder.

Print an email

Sometimes you'll need to print an email or its attachment. Print is not an option on the toolbar though. You can add it by right-clicking the toolbar and selecting Customize toolbar. If you don't see a Print icon and you don't want to add one, you can click the Alt key on the keyboard, click File and then click Print.

1. Select the email to print by clicking it in the Message pane.

2. Click Alt on the keyboard to show the Menu bar.

3. Click File and click Print.

4. In the Print dialogue box, select the printer to use if more than one exists.

5. Click Print. You can configure print preferences and choose what pages to print using Preferences. Refer to your printer's user manual to find out what print options your printer supports.

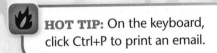
HOT TIP: On the keyboard, click Ctrl+P to print an email.

HOT TIP: You should see a printer icon appear on the right side of the taskbar during the print task. Click it for more information.

Apply a junk mail filter

Just like you receive unwanted information from phone solicitors, radio stations and television ads, you're going to get unwanted advertisements in emails. This is referred to as junk email or spam. Most of these advertisements are scams and rip-offs, and they also often contain pornographic images. There are four filtering options in Windows Live Mail: No Automatic Filtering, Low, High and Safe List Only.

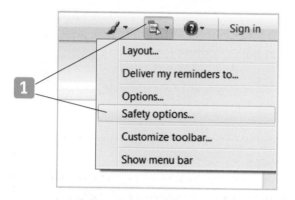

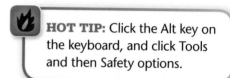

HOT TIP: Click the Alt key on the keyboard, and click Tools and then Safety options.

1 Click the Menus icon and click Safety options.

2 From the Options tab, make a selection.

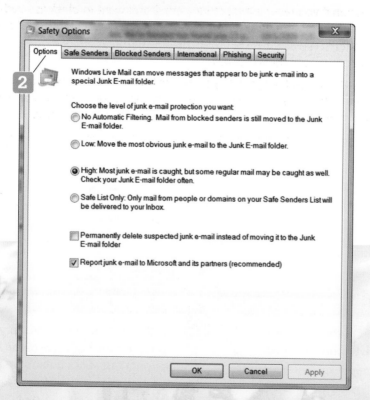

3 Click the Phishing tab.

4 Select Protect my Inbox from messages with potential Phishing links. Additionally, move phishing email to the Junk e-mail folder.

5 Click OK.

 ALERT: Don't give your email address to any website, company or include it in any registration card, unless you're willing to receive junk email from them and their constituents.

 ALERT: Check the Junk E-mail folder often to make sure no legitimate email has been moved there.

▶ **SEE ALSO:** Recover email from the Junk e-mail folder, earlier in this chapter.

WHAT DOES THIS MEAN?

No Automatic Filtering: use this only if you do not want Windows Live Mail to block junk email messages. Windows Live Mail will continue to block messages from email addresses listed on the Blocked Senders list.

Low: use this option if you receive very little junk email. You can start here and increase the filter if it becomes necessary.

High: use this option if you receive a lot of junk email and want to block as much of it as possible. Use this option for children's email accounts. Note that some valid email will probably be blocked, so you'll have to review the Junk e-mail folder occasionally to make sure you aren't missing any email you want to keep.

Safe List Only: use this option if you only want to receive messages from people or domain names on your Safe Senders list. This is a drastic step, and requires you to add every sender you want to receive mail from to the Safe Senders list. Use this as a last resort.

Create a folder

It's important to perform some housekeeping chores once a month or so. If you don't, Windows Live Mail may get bogged down and perform more slowly than it should, or you may be unable to manage the email you want to keep. One way you can keep Mail under control is to create a new folder to hold email you want to keep and move mail into it.

1 Click the arrow next to New, and click Folder.

2 Type a name for the new folder.

3 Select any folder. The folder you create will appear underneath it.

4 Click OK.

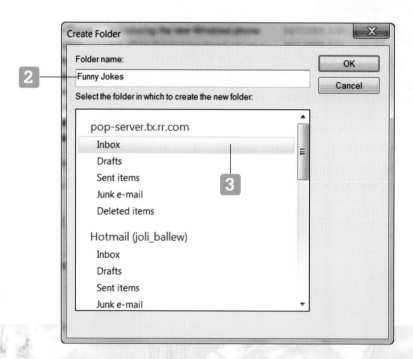

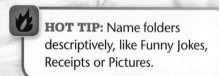

HOT TIP: Name folders descriptively, like Funny Jokes, Receipts or Pictures.

? DID YOU KNOW?
Using the same technique, you can create subfolders inside folders you create.

Move email to a folder

Moving an email from one folder (like your Inbox) to another (like Funny Jokes) is a simple task. Just drag the email from one folder to the other.

1 Click the email message to move in the Message pane.

2 Hold down the mouse button while dragging the message to the new folder.

3 The email will no longer be in the Inbox, but will be in the new folder.

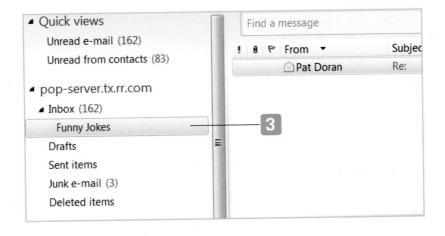

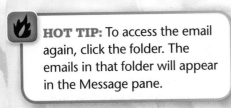

HOT TIP: To access the email again, click the folder. The emails in that folder will appear in the Message pane.

Delete email in a folder

In order to keep Mail from getting bogged down, you'll need to delete email in folders often. Depending on how much email you get, this may be as often as once a week.

1 Right-click Junk e-mail.

2 Click Empty 'Junk e-mail' folder.

3 Right-click Deleted items.

4 Click Empty 'Deleted items' folder.

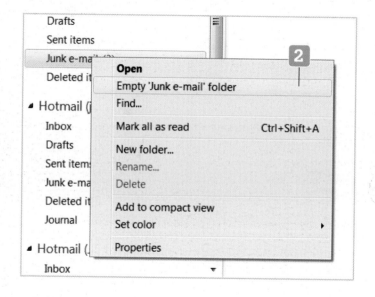

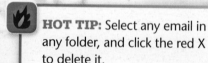

HOT TIP: Select any email in any folder, and click the red X to delete it.

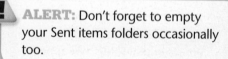

ALERT: Don't forget to empty your Sent items folders occasionally too.

7 Explore Office Live Workspace

Introduction

Office Live Workspace is a free workspace offered by Microsoft. You can use this workspace to save data like documents, presentations, spreadsheets and more. You can opt to use the space as a simple storing option, or you can share the data with others. Whatever you decide, Office Live Workspace can be used as your personal, virtual storage area, allowing you to easily create backups and to then access the data from any computer that offers Internet access.

Understand why online storage is crucial

Netbooks are very small, which makes them easy to lose and makes them more likely to be stolen (vs. desktop PCs). This is why it's crucial you learn to store data online, and not on your netbook. If you store data online, if your netbook is stolen or lost, you still have access to all of your data. In addition to this, there are other reasons why online storage is a good option for your netbook's data:

- You no longer have to carry around and keep up with a flash drive for backing up or transferring data.
- You can easily collaborate with others by sharing your online storage space.
- You can access the stored data from any computer with Internet access.

 HOT TIP: Instead of emailing yourself a file for use on another computer, upload it to your online storage site.

 DID YOU KNOW?
Online storage is protected with your user name and password. No one can access the data but you, unless you opt to share the space with others.

Get to know Office Live Workspace

To use Office Live Workspace, you'll need a Live ID. If you still don't have one, go to www.windowslive.com and click Get a Windows Live ID. Once you have a Live ID, you're ready to open your first workspace.

1 Use Internet Explorer and go to http://workspace.officelive.com.

2 Click Get Started Now.

3 Type your Windows Live email address (Live ID). Click Next.

4 Type your password, and click Sign in. The next time you visit Windows Live Workspace all you have to do is sign in.

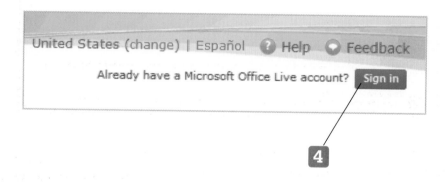

United States (change) | Español   ? Help   Feedback

Already have a Microsoft Office Live account?   Sign in

4

HOT TIP: Online applications change often due to application upgrades and version changes. What you see here may differ slightly from what you see on your computer.

Create a workspace

Once you're logged in you can easily create a workspace by following the directions given on the site, or here.

1 Click Create a workspace now.

2 Choose the kind of workspace to create.

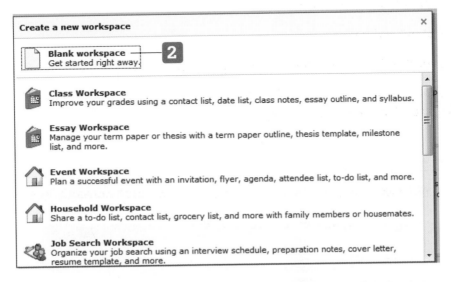

3 Name your workspace. Note that when you choose a workspace type, some documents are already created for you to fill in with your personalised information.

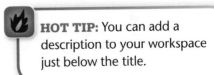

HOT TIP: You can add a description to your workspace just below the title.

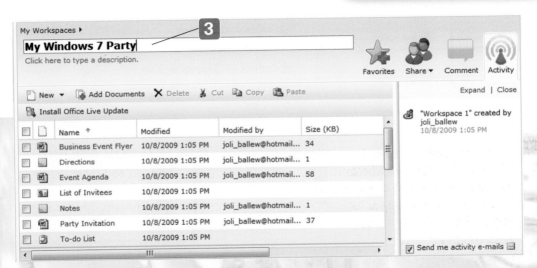

Add documents to your workspace

You can add documents to your workspace by clicking Add Documents. Upload multiple files by holding down the Ctrl key while clicking the files to add.

1 Click Add Documents.

2 Browse to a file to upload, click it and click Open.

3 The file will appear in your workspace, under the last item currently in the list.

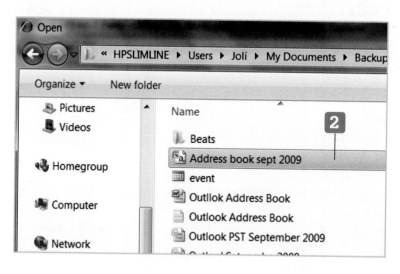

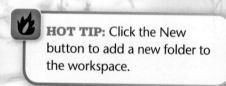
HOT TIP: Click the New button to add a new folder to the workspace.

DID YOU KNOW?
You can add more than documents. You can add spreadsheets, photos and even music.

Share your workspace

If you want to collaborate with others through your workspace, by allowing them to work with files you've placed there, you want to share the workspace.

1 Click Share.

2 Add the email addresses of the people you want to invite. Invite people as 'editors', and they can view and change data. Invite people as 'viewers' and they can only view data.

3 Type a personal message, if desired.

4 Configure additional options, such as letting people view the message without signing in, or to send yourself a copy of the invitation.

5 Click Send.

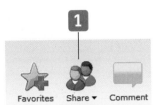

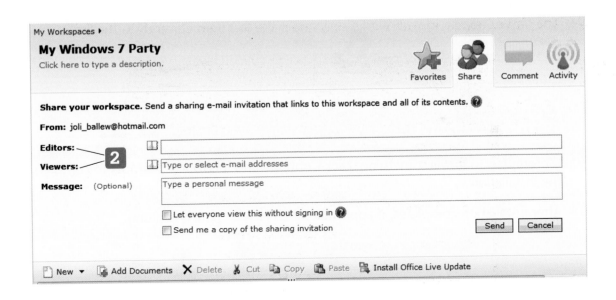

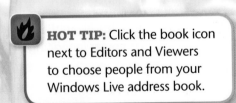

HOT TIP: Click the book icon next to Editors and Viewers to choose people from your Windows Live address book.

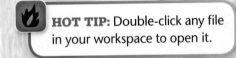

HOT TIP: Double-click any file in your workspace to open it.

Open a document in your workspace

The documents in your workspace, even those you did not add, are available for editing. You'll see different documents based on the type of workspace you created.

1 Double-click any file in the workspace.

2 Click Edit to make changes to the document.

3 If prompted to install something, click Continue and follow the prompts to complete the installation.

4 After installation completes, if applicable, the file will open for editing.

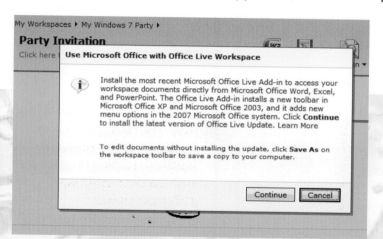

Install Office Live Update

If you use any Microsoft Office products, you should get Office Live Update. When used with Office Live Workspace, you can save the documents, spreadsheets and presentations you create in Microsoft Office directly back to your workspace. You won't ever have to save the data to your netbook again, if you don't want to.

1 In your workspace, locate Install Office Live Update and click it.

2 Click Run, and click Yes to verify the installation should proceed.

3 Complete any additional installation tasks, as required.

HOT TIP: It's a good idea to save data to an online Internet server. If your netbook is stolen, your documents and data won't be.

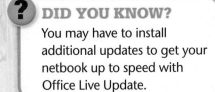

DID YOU KNOW?
You may have to install additional updates to get your netbook up to speed with Office Live Update.

Create a new Word document from inside your workspace

When you're working online and inside your workspace, you can create a new Word document using the available online tools. To create a new Word document:

1 Sign into your workspace and select your workspace.

2 Click the arrow next to New.

3 Choose Word document.

4 Your version of Microsoft Word will open where you can create the new document.

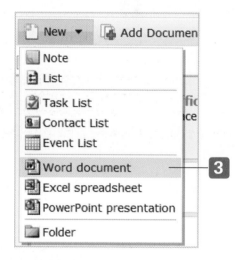

HOT TIP: If you've installed the Office Live Assistant, when you click Save or Save As, the document will save back to your workspace by default, not to your netbook.

? DID YOU KNOW?
With Office Live Update installed, clicking Save will save changes back to your workspace.

Open an Excel file saved in your workspace

If you've saved files to your workspace, you can easily view them by double-clicking. One type of file you can view is an Excel file.

1 Log into your workspace and double-click an Excel file stored there. (You may not have one, but if you do, proceed.)

2 Double-click the Excel file to open it.

3 View the Excel file in your web browser.

4 Click Edit to edit the file. You'll need to have installed the required software, detailed earlier, to perform edits.

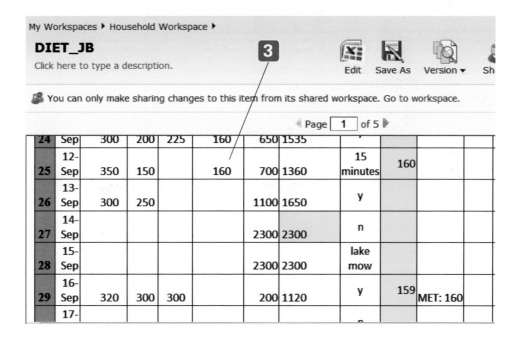

 HOT TIP: You'll have to log in again the first time you open a file for editing on your netbook.

 DID YOU KNOW? Click Activity to view recent activity within your workspace.

Save a PowerPoint presentation to your workspace

Just as is possible with Word and Excel, after installing the Office Live Update, you can save any new PowerPoint presentation to your workspace. To save a presentation to a workspace:

1 Open Microsoft PowerPoint on your netbook.

2 Open or create a PowerPoint presentation.

3 Click the Office button and point to Save to Office Live.

4 Choose the workspace to save to.

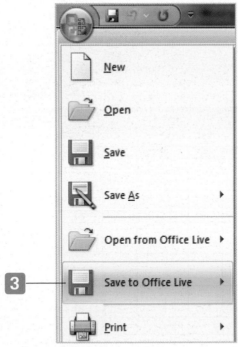

8 Use your built-in webcam

Introduction

Your netbook probably came with a built-in webcam; most netbooks do. The webcam may have even come with its own software for using it, but you'll still want to obtain a program for video chatting with your contacts. There are a lot of instant messaging programs to choose from, including those from familiar names like Yahoo!, AIM and Skype. However, because you've probably already obtained a Windows Live ID and downloaded Windows Live Messenger, in this chapter we'll focus on that.

Discover your webcam

It's best to find out first of all whether or not you have a webcam. If you can see a small lens at the top of your netbook, just above the computer screen, you do. If you can't see that or aren't sure, you can open the Devices and Printers window to find out.

1 Click Start.

2 Click Devices and Printers.

3 If you see an icon for a webcam, it's installed.

> **? DID YOU KNOW?**
> The Devices and Printers window shows the hardware installed on your netbook, including speakers, mice and even remote control devices.

> **HOT TIP:** Double-click the webcam icon to see if it is functioning correctly.

Get to know Windows Live Messenger

The best option for video messaging is Windows Live Messenger, and you may have already downloaded it. With Windows Live Messenger you can:

1 Instantly communicate using text, voice or video with anyone who has a compatible instant messaging program.

2 Share personal files, photos and videos using a Shared Folder.

3 Make phone calls to friends, family and contacts without paying long distance.

4 Make video calls or PC-to-PC calls to anyone with a messenger account.

5 Send your video to contacts even if they do not have their own video camera.

 HOT TIP: If you don't have Windows Live Messenger, go to www.download.live.com to get it.

? DID YOU KNOW?
You may already have Windows Live Messenger if you've worked through this book from the beginning. Click Start, All Programs and Windows Live to find out.

Open Windows Live Messenger

There are several ways to open Live Messenger, and it may already be open and available from the taskbar. Here's the quadruple-click option:

1 Click Start.

2 Click All Programs.

3 Click Windows Live.

4 Click Windows Live Messenger.

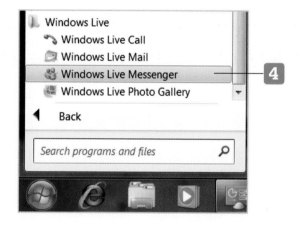

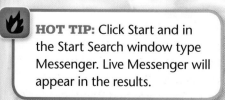

HOT TIP: Click Start and in the Start Search window type Messenger. Live Messenger will appear in the results.

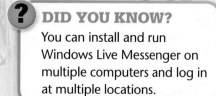

DID YOU KNOW?
You can install and run Windows Live Messenger on multiple computers and log in at multiple locations.

Sign into Windows Live Messenger

To use Windows Live Messenger you'll need a Windows Live ID. If you've been following along, you should already have one. If you don't, just click Sign up in the Windows Live Messenger start-up screen.

1 Open Windows Live Messenger.

2 Type your Windows Live ID in the email address field.

3 Type your password and configure options as desired. (If you don't see all of these options now, you will the next time you log in.)

4 Click Sign in. It is worth noting that instant messaging and video messaging take place over the Internet. Video quality is directly proportional to the speed of your Internet connection.

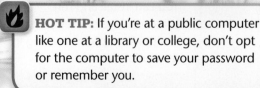 **HOT TIP:** If you're at a public computer like one at a library or college, don't opt for the computer to save your password or remember you.

Personalise Windows Live Messenger

There are a few specific things you can do to make the Live Messenger interface easier to navigate. There are also steps you can take to personalise it. The first thing you'll want to do is to show the Menu bar.

1 Open and sign into Windows Live Messenger.

2 Click the down arrow for Show Menu.

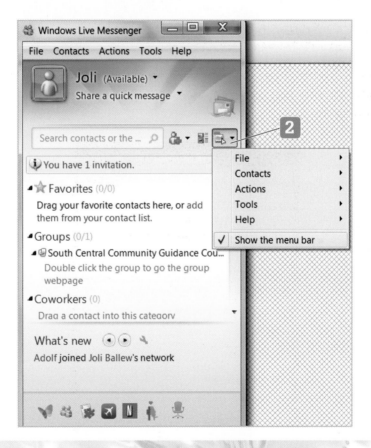

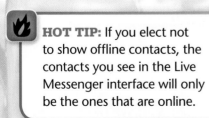

HOT TIP: If you elect not to show offline contacts, the contacts you see in the Live Messenger interface will only be the ones that are online.

3 Click Show the menu bar. (A tick will appear by the option.)

4 Click the Show Menu icon again.

5 Click the Change contact list layout icon. (It's to the left of the Show Menu icon.)

6 In the resulting dialogue box, make any desired changes. You may want to come back to this later after adding some contacts.

7 Click OK.

 HOT TIP: Explore the other tabs, especially Personal, Sign In and Alerts.

Run the Audio and Video Tuning Wizard

You need to run the Audio and Video Tuning Wizard to set up your webcam to work with Windows Live Messenger. You'll also need to configure your microphone and speakers. Don't worry, a wizard will walk you through it.

1 Open Windows Live Messenger and log in.

2 Click Tools, then click Audio and video setup.

3 Click Test to test your speakers, and then speak into the microphone to verify it is working properly. Click Next.

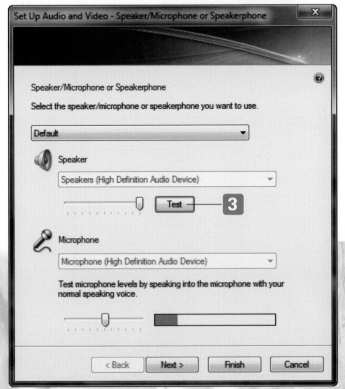

HOT TIP: If you can't see the Tools menu shown here, click the Alt key on your keyboard.

4 Select your webcam from the list. You should see yourself in it.

5 Click Webcam Settings to configure additional options.

6 Click OK and Finish.

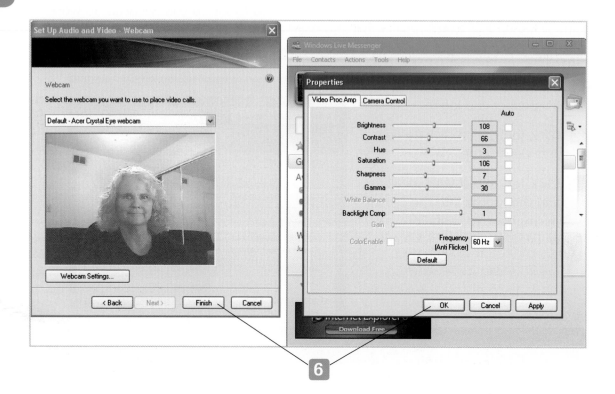

Add a contact

You can't have a video conversation with anyone until you add them as a contact! You add a contact using their instant messaging address. (You'll have to ask them for that.)

1 Click Contacts and then click Add a contact.

2 Type the information required and click Next.

3 Type a message if desired and click Send invitation.

4 As soon as the contact accepts your invitation, you'll see them in your Contacts list.

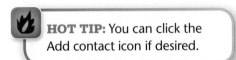

HOT TIP: You can click the Add contact icon if desired.

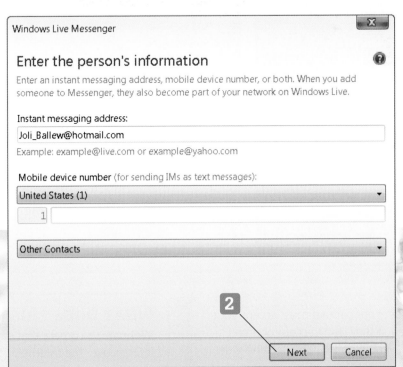

Have a video conversation

If you've worked through this chapter from the beginning and you've successfully added a contact, you're ready to have a video messaging conversation.

1 Open Windows Live Messenger and log in.

2 Double-click a contact in your contact list who is online and who has the required hardware to hold a voice conversation (microphone, speakers and/or headphones).

3 Click Video.

4 Wait while the contact accepts your video call.

5 During the call, the contact will see your webcam. If the recipient has a webcam, you will see theirs.

6 As with a voice call, either person can click Hang up to end the call.

WHAT DOES THIS MEAN?
Webcam: a camera that can send live images over the Internet.

9 Work with media

Introduction

Your Windows 7 netbook comes with lots of ways to enjoy media. It includes Media Player to listen to and manage music, and Media Center for viewing Internet TV, pictures, videos and additional media types (like online media). With the required hardware, you can even watch live TV. It does not come with a photo-editing and management program though, but you've already downloaded and installed Windows Live Photo Gallery, so you're all set!

Open Media Player and locate music

You open Media Player the same way you open other programs, from the Start menu. Once opened, you'll need to know where the Library button is, so you can access different kinds of media. We'll start with music.

1 Open Media Player from the taskbar.

2 Click the arrow next to the Library button.

3 Click Music.

ALERT: The first time you start Windows Media Player, you'll be prompted to set it up. Choose Express to accept the default settings.

? DID YOU KNOW?

Music is the default selection, but to be on the safe side, you should know how to change libraries. Did you notice Videos, Pictures, Recorded TV, Other Media and Playlists?

? DID YOU KNOW?

If you don't see a Library icon, click the arrow that will be there in its place.

Listen to a song

To play any music track, simply navigate to it and double-click it. Artist, Album and Genre are located in the 'Navigation' pane.

1 Open Media Player, if necessary, click the Library button and choose Music.

2 Click Album. (Note you can also click Artist or Genre.)

3 Double-click any album to play it.

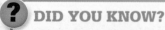

DID YOU KNOW?

Media Player has Back and Forward buttons you can use to navigate Media Player.

4 Double-click any song on the album to play it. Note the controls at the bottom of the screen.

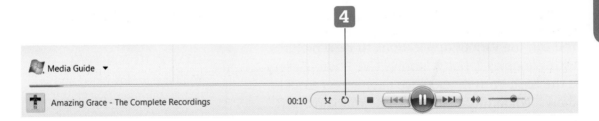

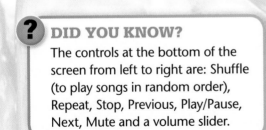

DID YOU KNOW?

The controls at the bottom of the screen from left to right are: Shuffle (to play songs in random order), Repeat, Stop, Previous, Play/Pause, Next, Mute and a volume slider.

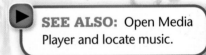

SEE ALSO: Open Media Player and locate music.

View pictures in Windows Live Photo Gallery

You can use various applications to view pictures with Windows 7, but Windows Live Photo Gallery is the best. With it, you have easy access to slide shows, editing tools and picture groupings. You can sort and filter and organise as desired.

1 Open Windows Live Photo Gallery. If prompted, log in using your Windows Live ID.

2 Notice the sample pictures. Double-click any picture to open it in a larger window.

3 Click Back to Gallery to return to the previous page.

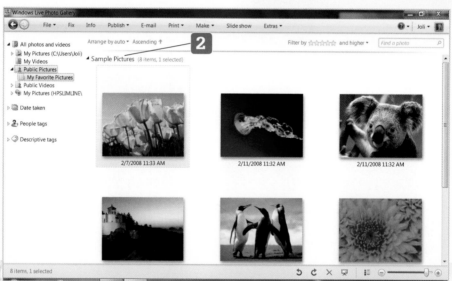

Play a slide show of pictures

1 Open Windows Live Photo Gallery.

2 Select any folder that contains pictures.

3 Click the Slide Show button. Wait at least three seconds.

4 To end the show, press the Esc key on the keyboard.

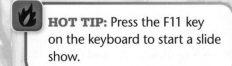

HOT TIP: Press the F11 key on the keyboard to start a slide show.

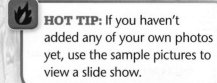

HOT TIP: If you haven't added any of your own photos yet, use the sample pictures to view a slide show.

Auto adjust picture quality

With pictures now on your netbook and available in Windows Live Photo Gallery, you can perform some editing. Photo Gallery offers the ability to correct brightness and contrast, colour temperature, tint and saturation, among other things.

1 Open Windows Live Photo Gallery.

2 Double-click a picture to edit.

3 Click Fix.

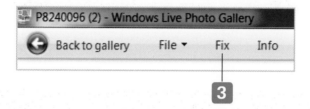

4 Click Auto adjust to fix problems with the photo. Adjustments will be made automatically.

5 Continue adjusting as desired, using the sliders to adjust the settings.

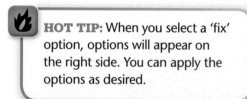 **HOT TIP:** When you select a 'fix' option, options will appear on the right side. You can apply the options as desired.

ALERT: After applying any option, to see more options, click the down and up arrows that will appear in the right pane.

 HOT TIP: Click the Back to Gallery button and your changes will be saved automatically.

Crop a picture

To crop means to remove parts of a picture you don't want by allowing you to reposition the picture and remove extraneous parts. You can also rotate the frame.

1 Open Photo Gallery.

2 Select a picture to crop.

3 Click Fix.

4 Click Crop Picture.

5 Drag the corners of the box to resize it, and drag the entire box to move it around in the picture.

6 Click Apply.

HOT TIP: Click the arrow next to Custom to apply a preconfigured size.

HOT TIP: Click Rotate frame to change the position of the crop box.

Open Media Center

Before you open Media Center for the first time, make sure you have a working Internet connection, speakers, and a CD/DVD drive. To access all of the features, purchase and install a TV tuner. (Only then can you watch live TV.)

1 Click Start.

2 Click Windows Media Center. (If it's not there, click All Programs to find it.).

3 Use the arrow keys on the keyboard to move through the options on the Media Center screen.

HOT TIP: Media Center's interface includes several menus: TV, Movies, Sports, Tasks, Extras, Pictures + Videos and Music. (You'll also find Media Center from Start and All Programs.)

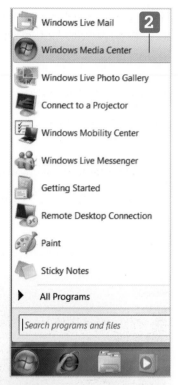

Explore Internet TV

Since you're exploring Media Center on a netbook, you probably won't have a TV tuner to watch live TV. However, you can watch Internet TV. You'll find this option under Extras.

1 Open Media Center.

2 Use the arrow keys on your keyboard to locate TV and Internet TV.

3 Click Install to access programming.

4 When installation completes, and this is a one-time task, browse programming options.

? DID YOU KNOW?

Media Center offers Back and Forward buttons to help you navigate the interface. Just position your mouse in the top left corner to see them.

View pictures in Media Center

You know you can view pictures in Photo Gallery and listen to music in Media Player, but you can do all of that in Media Center too. To view pictures, navigate to Pictures + Videos, for music, navigate to Music.

1 Open Media Center.

2 Use the arrow keys on the keyboard to locate Pictures + Videos.

3 Click picture library.

4 If you are connected to your home network and want to add pictures from other computers, click Add Pictures.

5 Work through the wizard to add the photos.

6 Select any photo folder to view its contents.

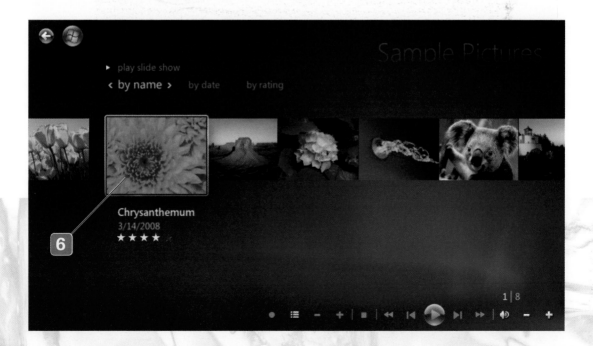

10 Connect to your home network

Introduction

If you have a home network, you will want to add your new Windows 7 netbook to it. Once you've joined the network you can use your netbook to access shared resources like printers and folders, share media you've acquired on your netbook, and access media on your home PC. You can use a network resource like a PC or external hard drive for backup too. Of course, you can access your home network's Internet connection as well.

Create the connection

When you connect a new PC running Windows 7 to a wired network or get within range of a wireless one, Windows 7 will find the network and then ask you what kind of network it is. It's a public network if you're in a coffee shop, library or cafe, and it's a private network if it's a network you manage, like one already in your home.

1 Connect physically to a wired network using an Ethernet cable or, if you have wireless hardware installed in your netbook, get within range of a wireless network.

2 Select Home, Work or Public location.

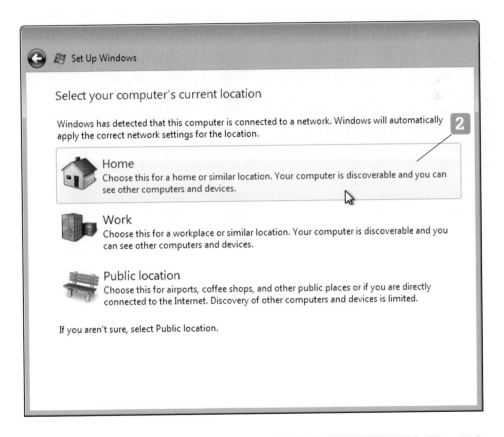

? **DID YOU KNOW?**

Connecting to an existing network allows you to access shared features of the network. In a coffee shop that's probably only a connection to the Internet; if it's a home network, it's your personal, shared data (and probably a connection to the Internet too).

WHAT DOES THIS MEAN?

Home: choose this if the network is your home network or a network you trust (like a network at a friend's house). This connection type lets your computer *discover* other PCs, printers and devices on the network, and they can see you.

Work: choose this if you are connecting to a network at work. The settings for Work and Home are the same, only the titles differ so you can tell them apart easily.

Public Network Location: choose this if the network you want to connect to is open to anyone within range of it, like networks in coffee shops, airports and libraries. Windows 7 figures if you choose Public, you only want to connect to the Internet and nothing else. It closes down *discoverability*, so that even your shared data is safe.

 HOT TIP: When a network is accessible, either because you've connected to it using an Ethernet cable or through a wireless network card inside your PC, the Set Network Location Wizard will appear.

 ALERT: If you're connecting to a wireless network at home, make sure wireless features are enabled on your netbook.

Enable Network Discovery

Network Discovery tells Windows 7 that you're interested in seeing, and possibly joining, other networks. With a netbook, you may want to connect to a public network in your local coffee house or a private one in your home.

1 Open the Network and Sharing Center.

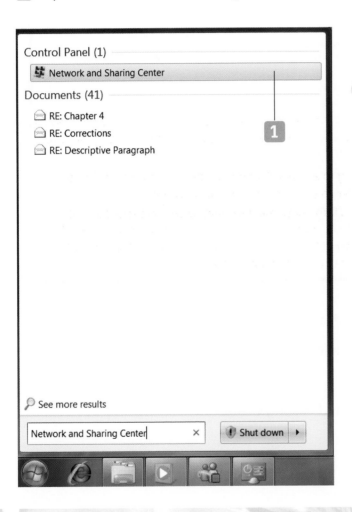

> **!** **ALERT:** If you're having trouble connecting to your home network or any public one, turning on Network Discovery manually will likely resolve the problem.

> **!** **ALERT:** You will have to enable Network Discovery to be able to view and ultimately join available networks.

> **?** **DID YOU KNOW?**
> The Network and Sharing Center is also where you set up file sharing, public folder sharing, printer sharing, password protected sharing and media sharing.

2 Notice the network map. It should show you are connected to a network and the Internet.

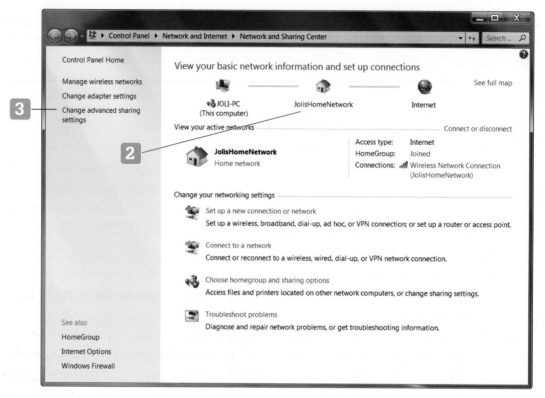

3 In the Tasks pane, click Change advanced sharing settings.

4 Click Turn on network discovery unless it is already turned on.

5 Click Save changes.

6 Click the X to close the Network and Sharing Center.

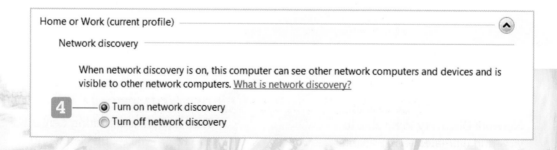

Verify sharing is enabled

When you tell Windows 7 you are joining a private network, like one at work or home, and you enable Network Discovery, certain sharing settings are configured. You need to see what sharing settings are configured and what options are not. You can then decide exactly how and what you want to share with others on your network.

1 Open the Network and Sharing Center.

2 In the Tasks pane, click Change advanced sharing settings.

3 Browse the sharing options. Turn on any options desired. You can turn on or turn off:

Control Panel Home

Manage wireless networks

Change adapter settings

2—Change advanced sharing settings

- File and printer sharing – files and printers on your netbook that you have shared can be accessed by others on the network.

- Public folder sharing – public folders on your netbook can be accessed by others on the network.

- Media streaming – media on your netbook can be accessed by people and computers on the network. Your netbook can also find media on the network.

- Password protected sharing – people who want to access your shared resources must have a user account and password to access them. If you turn this off, no validation is required.

- Homegroup connections – if you have other Windows 7 PCs on your network, you can create a Homegroup to more easily share data. Click to allow if this is the case.

4 Click Save changes.

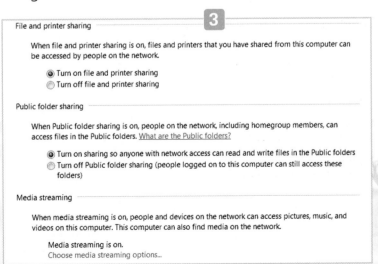

File and printer sharing

When file and printer sharing is on, files and printers that you have shared from this computer can be accessed by people on the network.

◉ Turn on file and printer sharing
○ Turn off file and printer sharing

Public folder sharing

When Public folder sharing is on, people on the network, including homegroup members, can access files in the Public folders. What are the Public folders?

◉ Turn on sharing so anyone with network access can read and write files in the Public folders
○ Turn off Public folder sharing (people logged on to this computer can still access these folders)

Media streaming

When media streaming is on, people and devices on the network can access pictures, music, and videos on this computer. This computer can also find media on the network.

Media streaming is on.
Choose media streaming options...

Save data to the Public folder

If you've enabled Public folder sharing, you'll want to save data to share in the Public folders.

1 Open a picture, document, or other item you wish to save to the Public folders.

2 Click File, then click Save As, Make a Copy, or a similar command.

3 In the resulting dialogue box, click Public.

4 Select the Public subfolder to save to.

5 Type a name for the file.

6 Click Save.

ALERT: In Windows Photo Gallery, you'll click File and Make a Copy.

HOT TIP: Save pictures to the Public Pictures folder. Save documents to the Public Documents folder.

 DID YOU KNOW?
It's actually better to move data you want to share into the Public folders. That way, you won't create duplicate copies of the data on your hard drive.

 HOT TIP: To move data, right-click it while dragging it to its new location. Click Move Here after dropping it, when prompted.

Access the Public folder

You can save data to the Public folder to easily share data with others on your network. You can access the Public folder by browsing to it. You can also browse the network for Public folders on other networked PCs. If you've created multiple accounts on your netbook, every account holder can also access what's in the Public folder.

1 Click Start, then click Computer.

2 Double-click Local Disk (C:). (The letter you see here may differ.)

3 Double-click Users.

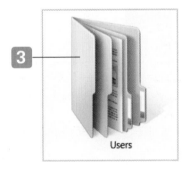

Users

4 If you think you'll use the Public folder often, right-click it and choose Send To, Desktop (create shortcut).

5 Double-click Public to open it.

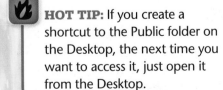

HOT TIP: If you create a shortcut to the Public folder on the Desktop, the next time you want to access it, just open it from the Desktop.

? DID YOU KNOW?
You can drag data from other open folders here to copy or move it. Right-click while dragging to have the option to move or copy.

Share a personal folder

If you don't want to use the Public folders, you can share data directly from your personal folders. To do this, you'll have to share the desired personal folders.

1 Locate the folder to share.

2 Right-click the folder.

3 Click Share with.

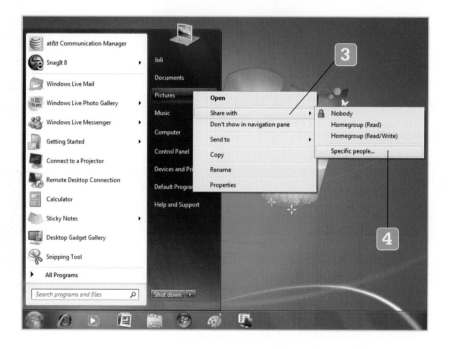

4 If you've created a HomeGroup, click the appropriate HomeGroup option. If not, choose Specific People.

5 Type the name of the person to share the folder with and click Add. Repeat this step to add more people.

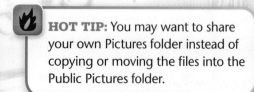 **HOT TIP:** You may want to share your own Pictures folder instead of copying or moving the files into the Public Pictures folder.

 HOT TIP: To set up a Homegroup, open the Network and Sharing Center and click Ready to Join next to Homegroup.

6 Click the arrow next to the new user name.

7 Select a sharing option.

8 Click Share.

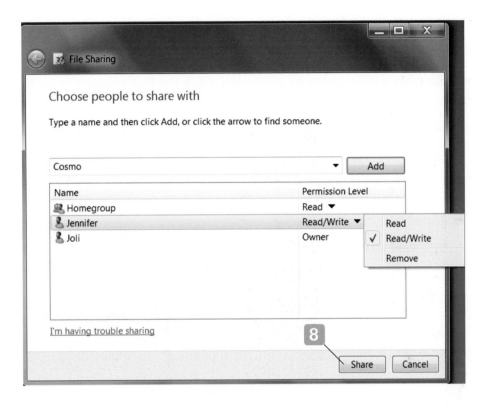

WHAT DOES THIS MEAN?

Owner: the person who created the file, uploaded the picture, purchased or ripped the music or saved the video.

Read: allows the user to access what's in the folder, but that user cannot edit it.

Read/Write: allows the user to access what's in the folder as well as edit it.

Rip: means to copy a CD to your hard drive.

Diagnose connection problems

If you are having trouble connecting to the Internet through a public or private network, you can diagnose Internet problems using the Network and Sharing Center.

1 Open the Network and Sharing Center.

2 To diagnose a nonworking Internet connection, click the red X.

3 Several solutions will probably be presented. Click the first solution to try to resolve the connectivity problem.

4 Often, the problem is resolved. If it is not, move to the next step and the next until it is.

5 Click the X in the top right corner of the Network and Sharing window to close it.

View your basic network information and set up connections

JOLI-PC
(This computer)

Internet

? DID YOU KNOW?
There are additional troubleshooting tips in the Help and Support pages. Click Start, then click Help and Support.

11 Install and manage hardware

Introduction

You can use your netbook with your existing devices just as you would with any computer. This means you can install your digital camera, printer or other hardware, and connect it when you want to use it. For obvious reasons you wouldn't leave a printer connected to your netbook all the time, but when you're at home and need access, you can certainly use it. If your netbook did not come with a webcam, it's easy enough to install one of those too. And if you use a communication method like Skype, which allows you to talk to others via your computer and Internet connection, you may want to install headphones as well.

To install a device you generally connect it, turn it on and wait while the driver installs. A driver is a piece of software (or code) that allows the device to communicate with Windows 7 and viceversa. You'll learn how Windows installs drivers automatically in this chapter, and how to manage installed devices easily.

Install a digital camera, webcam or insert a media card

Most of the time, adding a camera is a simple affair. You connect the camera to a USB port in the netbook, turn it on and wait for Windows 7 to install it. However, it's always best to have directions for performing a task, so in that vein, I've included them here.

1 Connect the camera to the netbook using either a USB cable or a FireWire cable. Turn on the camera.

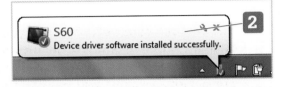

2 Wait while the driver is installed.

3 You'll see the camera in the Computer window (click Start, click Computer), as well as the Devices and Printers window, shown here.

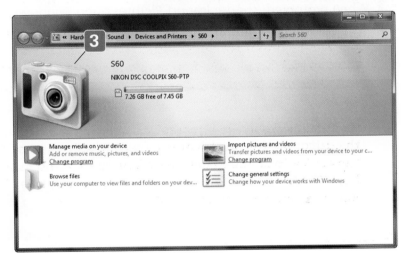

WHAT DOES THIS MEAN?

USB: a technology used to connect hardware to a computer. A USB cable is often used to connect a digital camera.

FireWire: a technology used to connect hardware to a computer. A FireWire cable is a cable often used to connect a digital video camera.

! ALERT: Your camera may have come with a CD. It's likely your netbook does not have a CD/DVD drive. Don't worry; Windows 7 installs devices successfully (and without the installation CD) 98 per cent of the time.

! ALERT: If the camera does not install properly, refer to Chapter 12 to install the driver from the camera's CD, or consider uploading pictures from the camera's media card and foregoing installation altogether.

Import pictures from a digital camera or media card

After you've taken pictures with your digital camera, you'll want to move or copy those pictures to your netbook. Once stored on the netbook's hard drive, you can view, edit, email or print the pictures (among other things). Here you'll learn how to import pictures to Windows Live Photo Gallery, part of the free Windows Live Essentials suite of applications.

1 Connect the device or insert the media card into the card reader. If applicable, turn on the camera.

2 When prompted, choose Import Pictures using Windows Live Photo Gallery.

3 Click Import all new items now.

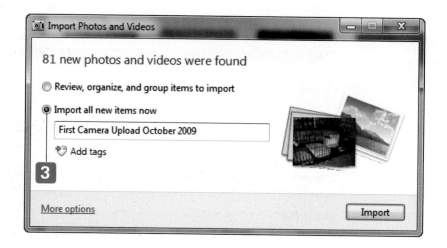

4 Type a descriptive name for the group of pictures you're importing and click Next.

? DID YOU KNOW?
These steps work for importing pictures from a mobile phone too.

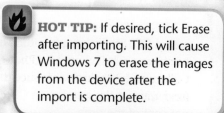

HOT TIP: If desired, tick Erase after importing. This will cause Windows 7 to erase the images from the device after the import is complete.

5 Wait while the import process completes.

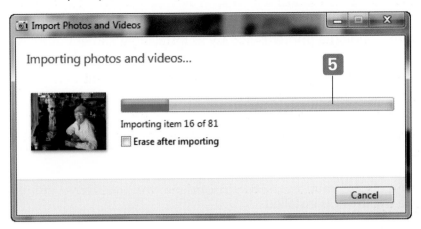

6 View your new photos.

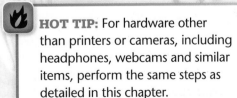

ALERT: If your device isn't recognised when you plug it in and turn it on, in Windows Live Photo Gallery click File, and click Import from Camera or Scanner.

HOT TIP: For hardware other than printers or cameras, including headphones, webcams and similar items, perform the same steps as detailed in this chapter.

Install a printer

Most of the time, adding a printer is as easy as installing a camera. And as with cameras, if you don't have a CD/DVD drive in your netbook, you'll have to hope that Windows 7 can install it automatically. Most of the time, it can.

1 Connect the printer to a wall outlet.

2 Connect the printer to the netbook using either a USB cable or a parallel port cable.

3 Turn on the printer.

4 Wait while the driver is installed.

5 Disconnect and turn off the printer when you aren't using it. There's no reason to leave it connected to your netbook.

6 You can view all connected and installed printers in the Devices and Printers window, shown here.

ALERT: While your printer will probably install without a problem, you may still need to install the printer's software to access advanced printer properties. If this turns out to be the case, refer to Chapter 12 to install it.

? DID YOU KNOW?
USB is a faster connection than a parallel port, but FireWire is faster than both.

What to do when the installation fails

If you've properly connected the hardware, turned it on, and Windows 7 cannot find the required driver, you'll see a message like this one. When that happens, you have a few options.

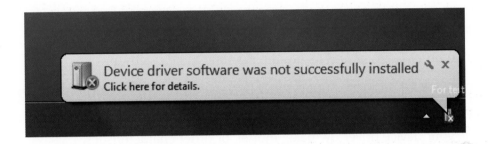

1 Let Windows look to the Internet for the proper driver. If prompted, connect to the Internet to see if Windows can resolve the problem.

2 Locate, download and install a compatible driver from the Internet yourself. Refer to the next section for instructions.

3 Install the software and driver from the CD or DVD that came with it. If your netbook does not have a CD/DVD drive, refer to Chapter 12.

ALERT: If the hardware does not install properly, consider returning it for something that will. Look for a logo that says the device is compatible with Windows 7.

 HOT TIP: Be careful when installing from a CD/DVD. Much of the software on it is stuff you don't need. Try to only install the driver. Later, if you deem it necessary, go back and install the software.

Locate a driver

As noted, almost all of the time, hardware installs automatically and with no input from you (other than plugging in the device and turning it on). However, in rare cases, the hardware does not install properly or is simply not available. If this happens, you'll be informed that the hardware did not install and may not work properly. If you cannot replace the device with something Windows 7 recognises, you'll have to locate and install the driver yourself.

1 Write down the name and model number of the device.

2 Open Internet Explorer and locate the manufacturer's website.

3 Locate a link for Support, Support and Drivers, Customer Support or something similar. Click it.

4 Locate your device driver by make, model, or other characteristics.

HOT TIP: The make and model of a device are probably located on the bottom of the device.

HOT TIP: To find the manufacturer's website, try putting a www. before the company name and a .com after. (www.epson.com, www.hewlett-packard.com and www.apple.com are examples.)

ALERT: Locating a driver is the first step. You must now download the driver, and later, install it.

Download and install a driver

If you've located the driver you need, you can now download and install it. Downloading is the process of saving the driver to your computer's hard drive. Once downloaded, you can install the driver.

1 Locate the driver as detailed in the previous section.

2 Click Download driver, Obtain software or something similar.

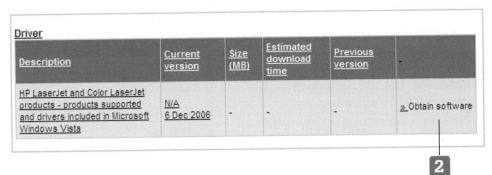

Driver

Description	Current version	Size (MB)	Estimated download time	Previous version	
HP LaserJet and Color LaserJet products - products supported and drivers included in Microsoft Windows Vista	N/A 6 Dec 2006	-	-	-	» Obtain software

3 Click Save.

4 Click Run, Install or Open Window to begin the installation.

5 Follow the directions in the set-up process to complete the installation.

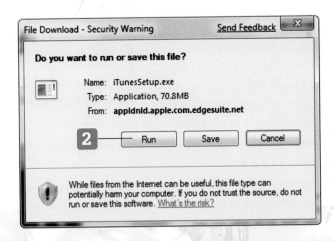

File Download - Security Warning   Send Feedback

Do you want to run or save this file?

Name: iTunesSetup.exe
Type: Application, 70.8MB
From: appldnld.apple.com.edgesuite.net

[Run]   [Save]   [Cancel]

While files from the Internet can be useful, this file type can potentially harm your computer. If you do not trust the source, do not run or save this software. What's the risk?

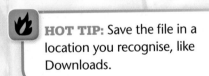

HOT TIP: Save the file in a location you recognise, like Downloads.

ALERT: If installation does not begin automatically, browse to the location of the file and double-click it to begin the installation manually.

Use ReadyBoost

ReadyBoost is a technology that lets you add more RAM (random access memory) to your netbook easily, without opening the case. Adding RAM often improves performance dramatically. ReadyBoost lets you use a USB flash drive or a secure digital memory card (like the one in your digital camera) as RAM, if it meets certain requirements.

1 Insert a USB flash drive, thumb drive, portable music player or memory card into an available slot on the outside of your netbook.

2 Wait while Windows 7 checks to see if the device can perform as memory.

3 If prompted to use the flash drive or memory card to improve system performance, click Speed up my system.

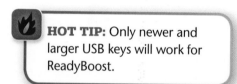 **HOT TIP:** Only newer and larger USB keys will work for ReadyBoost.

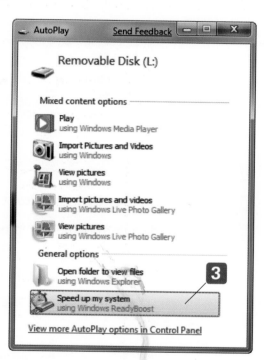

ALERT: USB keys must be at least USB 2.0 and have at least 64 MB of free space, but don't worry about that, you'll be told if the hardware isn't up to par.

WHAT DOES THIS MEAN?

RAM: Random Access Memory. RAM is where information is stored temporarily so the operating system has quick access to it. The more RAM you have, the better your computer should perform.

USB or thumb drive: a small device that plugs into a USB port on your netbook, often for the purpose of backing up or storing files on external media.

Portable music player: often a small USB drive. This device also has a headphone jack and controls for listening to music stored on it.

Media card: a removable card used in digital cameras to store data and transfer it to the computer.

Change when your netbook sleeps

Your netbook is configured to go to sleep after a specific period of idle time. You can change how long the computer is idle before going into sleep mode from the Power Options window.

1 Click Start and in the Start Search window type Power.

2 Under Control Panel, click Power Options.

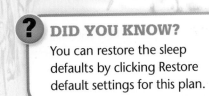

DID YOU KNOW?

You can restore the sleep defaults by clicking Restore default settings for this plan.

3 Click Change when the computer sleeps.

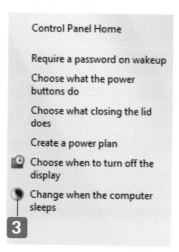

Control Panel Home

Require a password on wakeup

Choose what the power buttons do

Choose what closing the lid does

Create a power plan

Choose when to turn off the display

Change when the computer sleeps

3

4 Use the drop-down lists to make changes as desired.

5 Click Save changes.

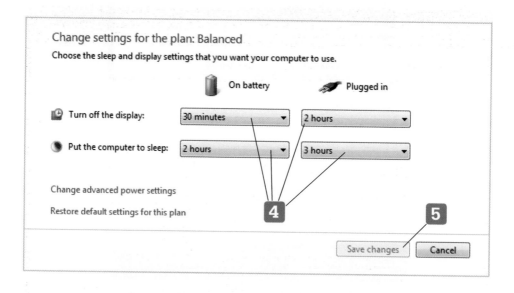

Change settings for the plan: Balanced
Choose the sleep and display settings that you want your computer to use.

	On battery	Plugged in
Turn off the display:	30 minutes	2 hours
Put the computer to sleep:	2 hours	3 hours

Change advanced power settings

Restore default settings for this plan

4

5

Save changes   Cancel

HOT TIP: When you change the options here, the changes are applied to the currently selected plan, in this case, Balanced.

Change what happens when you press the power button or close the lid

Your computer is configured to do something specific when you press the power button and when you close the netbook's lid. To view the default behaviour and change it if desired, look to the Power Options window once more.

1 Click Start, and in the Start Search window type Power.

2 In the results, under Programs, click Power Options.

3 Click Choose what the power buttons do.

4 Use the drop-down lists to make changes as desired.

5 Click Save changes.

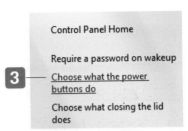

Control Panel Home

Require a password on wakeup

3 — Choose what the power buttons do

Choose what closing the lid does

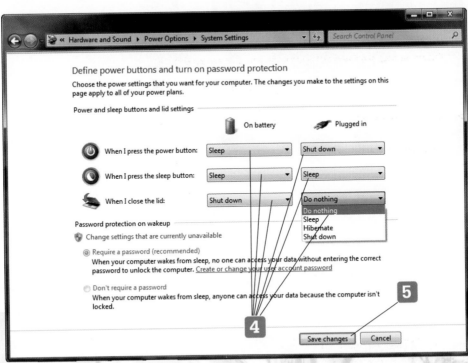

 HOT TIP: You can change the settings so that pressing the power button causes the computer to go to sleep.

 ALERT: Always shut down the computer when you aren't going to use it for a few days.

Manage all connected devices

There's one place you can view and manage all of your connected devices. From there, you can see what's working and what isn't, what's connected and what isn't, and what devices, like printers, are configured as default devices.

1 Click Start.

2 Click Devices and Printers. Some people call this window 'Device Stage'.

3 Review the hardware; double-click any device to view or edit its properties.

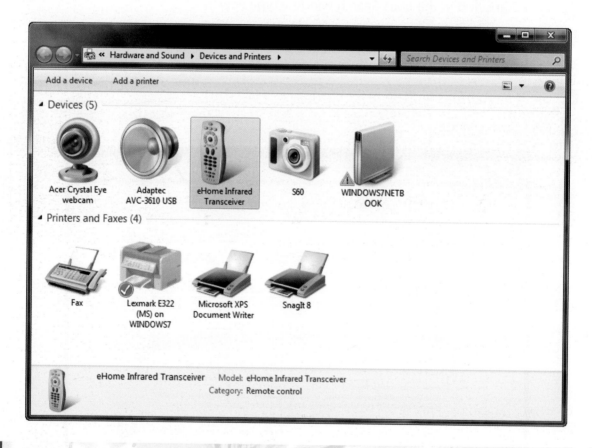

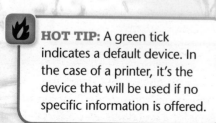

HOT TIP: A green tick indicates a default device. In the case of a printer, it's the device that will be used if no specific information is offered.

12 Install software on a CD or DVD

Introduction

You'll occasionally need to install software. This may be software you purchase online and download from the Internet, software you already own on CD or DVD, or software you obtain with a printer or camera. Much of the time, the software you want to install is on a CD or DVD.

Your netbook probably did not come with a CD or DVD drive though. Manufacturers, in general, have opted to leave drives out of netbooks. There are many reasons for this: a drive would make the netbook heavier, drain battery power and require the netbook to be thicker or larger, among other things.

So what happens then when you need to install a program, driver or application from a CD or DVD? Luckily, there are options. You can download and install the program (or a compatible one) from the Internet, use a shared drive from a networked computer, copy the installation files to a USB flash drive, or even install an external CD/DVD drive.

Explore installation options

As you can see from the chapter contents list, there are plenty of options for installing software currently on a disk. The easiest by far is to locate the program or driver on the Internet and download it to your netbook. However, if you have to use the CD or DVD, you do have options.

1. Share a networked computer's CD/DVD drive: share the CD/DVD drive on a networked PC. Browse to it from the netbook, and run the installation program from there. The network can be wired or wireless.

2. Copy the CD to a Network folder: copy the entire CD to a network folder you can access from the netbook. Browse to the folder to access the installation files.

3. Copy the CD to a USB flash drive: copy the entire CD to the flash drive using another computer, and then use the flash drive to install the software onto the netbook. Sometimes this method works and sometimes it doesn't.

4. Connect an External CD/DVD Drive: connect an external CD/DVD drive and install it. Run the installation program using this drive.

HOT TIP: Sharing a network disk drive is something that must be done on the PC that contains the drive.

ALERT: Copying the installation files to a flash drive won't work in all instances, for example to copy the installation files for an operating system.

Install software from the Internet

If you can find the program you want to install on the Internet, installation is as simple as downloading the product and following the prompts to install it. This is how you installed Windows Live Essentials in Chapter 5 and device drivers in Chapter 11.

1 Locate the program or driver to install.

2 Click the Download or Download Now button.

3 Click Run, then click Run again.

4 Work through the installation wizard.

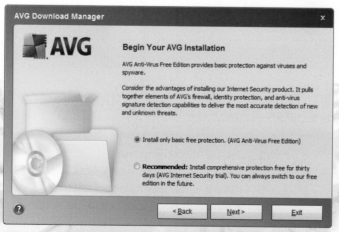

 **ALERT:** Only download and install software from reputable companies with good reviews. Downloaded software can contain malware or viruses.

HOT TIP: AVG Free is a free anti-virus program you can download from http://free.avg.com.

Share a networked CD/DVD drive

You can install a program that is on a disk from another computer on your network. The first step in doing so is to share the drive at that computer.

1 On the networked computer (not your netbook), click Start and click Computer (or My Computer).

2 Right-click the CD/DVD drive and click Share, Sharing or Sharing and Security (whichever is offered).

3 Locate the option to share the drive. You may have to click Advanced Sharing. The steps depend on what operating and file system the computer uses.

4 Click OK or Apply to save the changes.

? DID YOU KNOW?
After sharing a drive, you'll see an icon on it that shows it's shared.

Install software from a shared network CD/DVD drive

With the drive shared, installation is as easy as browsing to the drive and locating the installation icon.

1 On your netbook, click the folder icon on the taskbar.

2 Click Network, and click the computer the drive resides on.

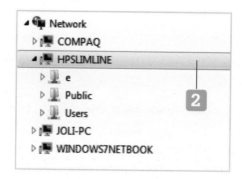

3 Double-click to open the shared drive, often D:, E:, or something similar.

4 Locate the installation program and run it.

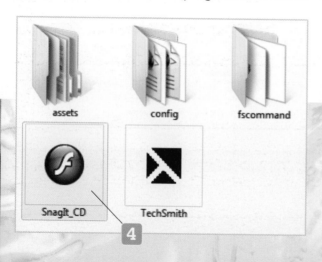

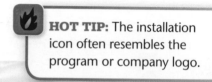

HOT TIP: The installation icon often resembles the program or company logo.

? DID YOU KNOW?

Installation over a network takes longer than installing from a CD or DVD on the same computer.

Copy the installation CD to a USB flash drive

Before you can install a program from a flash drive, you must first copy the files to it. You'll need to do that on a computer that has both an available USB slot and a CD/DVD drive.

1 Insert your flash drive.

2 Insert the CD.

3 Close any open dialogue boxes.

4 Open the Computer window.

5 Right-click the CD/DVD drive and select Open in new window.

6 Position the two windows so you can see both.

7 Select and drag all of the files on the CD/DVD to the flash drive.

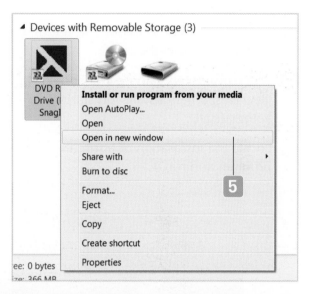

> ⚠ **ALERT:** Copy the entire CD to the flash drive, don't simply copy the installation program files.

Install software from a USB flash drive

Once the installation files are copied to a flash drive, all you have to do is insert the flash drive into an available slot on your netbook.

1 Insert the flash drive into a USB slot on the outside of your netbook.

2 When prompted, choose Open folder to view files, unless installation starts automatically.

3 Locate the installation or application program and run it.

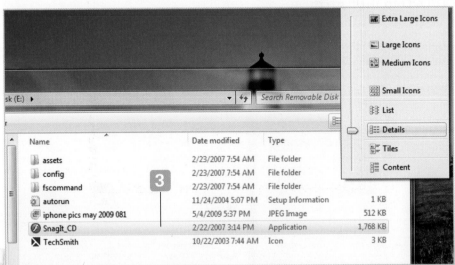

? DID YOU KNOW?

The first time you insert your flash drive you may have to wait a few seconds while it installs the new hardware.

🔥 HOT TIP: If you aren't sure which icon in the folder is the installation or application file, click the View button and select Details.

Install software from an external CD/DVD drive

Netbooks have USB ports, and an external CD/DVD drive can be connected using one. If you can get your hands on one of these drives by borrowing or buying it, you'll have an easy way to install software.

1 Plug the drive into an electrical outlet and to the netbook using the hardware supplied.

2 Wait while the drive installs.

3 Insert the CD or DVD into the external drive.

4 When the installation dialogue box appears, work through the installation wizard to install the program.

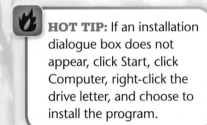 **HOT TIP:** If an installation dialogue box does not appear, click Start, click Computer, right-click the drive letter, and choose to install the program.

ALERT: If you encounter problems when running a program you installed from an external or network drive, you will have to uninstall the program, copy the disk to your netbook, and install the program from there. Some programs, especially those with clipart, will look to the disk for data.

13 Stay secure

Introduction

Windows 7 comes with a lot of built-in features to keep you and your data safe. Windows 7 security tools and features help you avoid email scams, harmful websites, and hackers, and also help you protect your data and your computer from unscrupulous coworkers or nosy family members. If you know how to take advantage of the available safeguards, you'll be protected in almost all cases. You just need to be aware of the dangers, heed security warnings when they are given (and resolve them), and use all of the available features in Windows 7 to protect yourself and your netbook.

Add a new user account

You created your user account when you first turned on your new Windows 7 netbook. Your user account is what defines your personal folders as well as your settings for desktop background, screen saver and other items. You are the 'administrator' of your computer. If you share the netbook with someone, they should have their own user account too.

1 Click Start.

2 Click Control Panel.

3 Click Add or remove user accounts.

4 Click Create a new account.

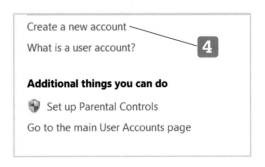

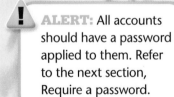

ALERT: If every person who accesses your netbook has their own standard user account and password, and if every person logs on using that account and then logs off the netbook each time they've finished using it, you'll never have to worry about anyone accessing anyone else's personal data.

ALERT: All accounts should have a password applied to them. Refer to the next section, Require a password.

5 Type a new account name, verify Standard user is selected, and click Create Account. It is worth noting that once the account is created you can also click Change the picture, Change the account name, Create a password (Remove the password) and other options to further personalise the account.

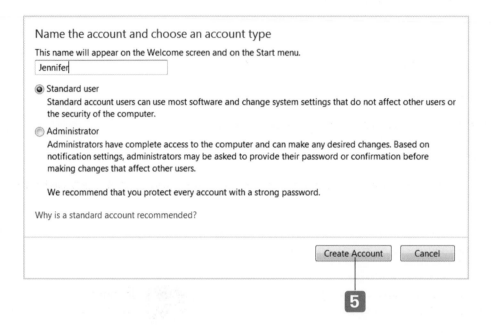

Name the account and choose an account type

This name will appear on the Welcome screen and on the Start menu.

Jennifer

◉ Standard user

Standard account users can use most software and change system settings that do not affect other users or the security of the computer.

◉ Administrator

Administrators have complete access to the computer and can make any desired changes. Based on notification settings, administrators may be asked to provide their password or confirmation before making changes that affect other users.

We recommend that you protect every account with a strong password.

Why is a standard account recommended?

[Create Account] [Cancel]

5

? DID YOU KNOW?

Administrators can make changes to system-wide settings but Standard users cannot (without an Administrator name and password).

Require a password

All user accounts, even yours, should be password-protected. When a password is configured, you must type the password to log onto your PC or laptop. This protects the PC from unauthorised access.

1 Click Start.

2 Click Control Panel.

3 Click Add or remove user accounts.

4 Click the user account to apply a password to.

5 Click Create a password.

6 Type the new password, type it again to confirm it, and type a password hint.

Make changes to Jennifer's account

Change the account name
Create a password ———————— **5**
Change the picture
Set up Parental Controls
Change the account type
Delete the account

Manage another account

Jennifer
Standard user

 **DID YOU KNOW?**
When you need to make a system-wide change, you have to be logged on as an administrator or type an administrator's user name and password.

! **ALERT:** Create a password that contains upper and lower case letters and a few numbers. Write the password down and keep it somewhere out of sight and safe.

7 Click Create password.

Create a password for Jennifer's account

Jennifer
Standard user

You are creating a password for Jennifer.

If you do this, Jennifer will lose all EFS-encrypted files, personal certificates and stored passwords for Web sites or network resources.

To avoid losing data in the future, ask Jennifer to make a password reset floppy disk.

New password

Confirm new password

If the password contains capital letters, they must be typed the same way every time.

How to create a strong password

Type a password hint

The password hint will be visible to everyone who uses this computer.

What is a password hint?

Create password   Cancel

7

Configure Windows Update

It's very important to configure Windows Update to get and install updates automatically. This is the easiest way to ensure your computer is as up-to-date as possible, at least as far as patching security flaws Microsoft uncovers, having access to the latest features, and obtaining updates to the operating system itself. I propose you verify that the recommended settings are enabled as detailed here, and occasionally check for optional updates manually.

1 Click Start.

2 Click Control Panel.

3 Click System and Security.

4 Under Windows Update, click Turn automatic updating on or off.

WHAT DOES THIS MEAN?

Windows Update: if enabled and configured properly, when you are online, Windows 7 will check for security updates automatically, and install them. You don't have to do anything, and your netbook is always updated with the latest security patches and features.

5 In the left pane, click Change Settings.

6 Configure the settings as shown here or verify settings are similar, and click OK.

6

Choose how Windows can install updates

When your computer is online, Windows can automatically check for important updates and install them using these settings. When new updates are available, you can also install them before shutting down the computer.

How does automatic updating help me?

Important updates

Install updates automatically (recommended)

Install new updates: Every day   at   3:00 AM

Recommended updates

☑ Give me recommended updates the same way I receive important updates

Who can install updates

☑ Allow all users to install updates on this computer

Microsoft Update

☑ Give me updates for Microsoft products and check for new optional Microsoft software when I update Windows

Software notifications

☐ Show me detailed notifications when new Microsoft software is available

Note: Windows Update might update itself automatically first when checking for other updates. Read our privacy statement online.

OK   Cancel

ALERT: You may see that optional components or updates are available. You can view these updates and install them if desired.

? DID YOU KNOW?
If the computer is not online at 3:00 a.m., it will check for updates the next time it is.

Scan for viruses with Windows Defender

You don't have to do much to Windows Defender except understand that it offers protection against Internet threats like malware. It's enabled by default and it runs in the background. However, if you ever think your computer has been attacked by an Internet threat (virus, worm, malware, etc.) you can run a manual scan here.

1 Open Windows Defender. (Click Start, type Defender, and in the results click Windows Defender.)

2 Click the arrow next to Scan (not the Scan icon). Click Full scan if you think the computer has been infected.

3 Click the X in the top right corner to close the Windows Defender window.

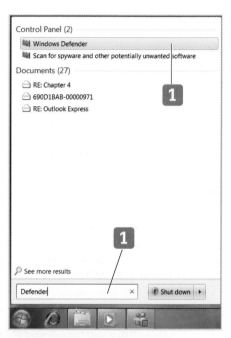

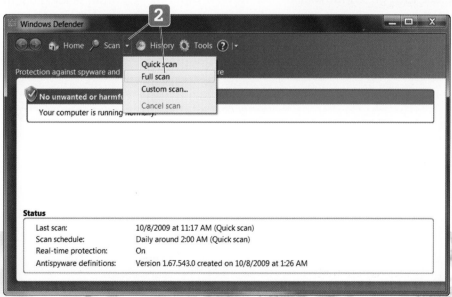

WHAT DOES THIS MEAN?

Malware: stands for malicious software. Malware includes viruses, worms, spyware, etc.

Enable the firewall

Windows Firewall is a software program that checks the data that comes in from the Internet (or a local network) and then decides whether it's good data or bad. If it deems the data harmless, it will allow it to come though the firewall, if not, it's blocked.

1 Click Start, and in the Start Search window type Firewall.

2 Click Windows Firewall.

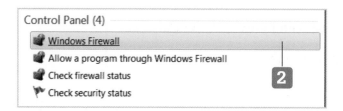

3 The firewall should be enabled, as shown here.

4 If it is not enabled
- From the left pane, click Turn Windows Firewall on or off.
- Select Turn on Windows Firewall. Review other settings.
- Click OK.

ALERT: You have to have a firewall to keep hackers from getting access to your netbook, and to help prevent your computer from sending out malicious code if it is ever attacked by a virus or worm.

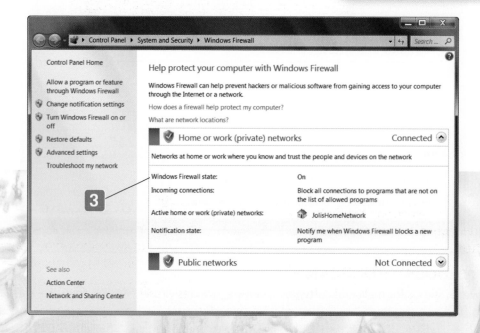

View and resolve Security Center warnings

Windows 7 tries hard to take care of your netbook and your data. You'll see a pop-up if your anti-virus software is out of date (or not installed), if you don't have the proper security settings configured, or if Windows Update or the firewall is disabled. You'll also get a user account control prompt each time you want to install a program or make a system-wide change.

1 In the taskbar, click the icon that looks like a flag.

2 Click Open Action Center.

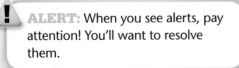

ALERT: When you see alerts, pay attention! You'll want to resolve them.

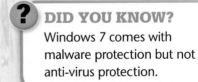

DID YOU KNOW?
Windows 7 comes with malware protection but not anti-virus protection.

3 If there's anything in red or yellow, click the down arrow (if necessary) to see the problem.

4 Click the suggestion button to view the resolution and perform the task. In this case, the button is View message details.

Review recent messages and resolve problems

Action Center has detected one or more issues for you to review.

Security   ⌄   **3**

Maintenance   ⌄

Address a problem with NVIDIA Graphics Driver

NVIDIA Graphics Driver has stopped working 1 time(s), last occurring   [View message details]   **4**
on 10/7/2009 3:44 PM. Steps are available for addressing this
problem.

Archive this message

Install your video card driver

A driver for your video card is available online.   [View message details]

Archive this message

If you don't see your problem listed, try one of these:

Troubleshooting
Find and fix problems

Recovery
Restore your computer to an
earlier time

ALERT: Install anti-virus software to protect your PC from viruses and worms.

WHAT DOES THIS MEAN?

Virus: a self-replicating program that infects computers with intent to do harm. Viruses often come in the form of an attachment in an email.

Worm: a self-replicating program that infects computers with intent to do harm. However, unlike a virus, it does not need to attach itself to a running program.

Create a basic backup

Windows 7 comes with a backup program you can use to back up your personal data. The backup program is located in the Backup and Restore Center.

1 Open Backup and Restore. (Click Start, type Backup.)

2 If you have performed a backup before, click Back up now. Wait while the backup completes.

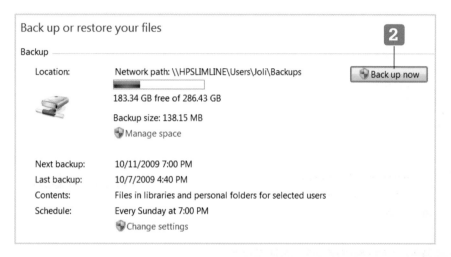

3 If you've never created a backup, click Set up backup.

- Decide on a place to save your backup.
- Click Save on a network and choose a location if desired.
- Select the backup destination.
- Click Next.

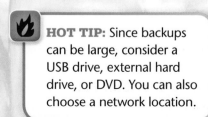

HOT TIP: Since backups can be large, consider a USB drive, external hard drive, or DVD. You can also choose a network location.

4 Select Let Windows choose (recommended).

5 Wait while the backup completes.

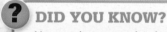

? DID YOU KNOW?

You can't create a backup on the hard disk of the computer you are backing up.

? DID YOU KNOW?

You may be prompted to insert a blank DVD, or insert a USB drive depending on the choice made in Step 3.

14 Fix problems

Introduction

When problems arise, you will want to resolve them quickly. Windows 7 offers plenty of help. System Restore can fix problems automatically by 'restoring' your computer to an earlier time. If the boot-up process is slow, you can disable unwanted start-up items with the System Configuration tool. Additionally, you can use the Network and Sharing Center to help you resolve connectivity problems and use Device Manager to 'roll back' a driver that didn't work, and if your computer seems bogged down, you can delete unwanted programs and files easily.

Use System Restore

System Restore regularly creates and saves *restore points* that contain information about your computer that Windows uses to work properly. If your computer starts acting funny, you can use System Restore to restore your computer to a time when the computer was working properly.

1 Open System Restore.

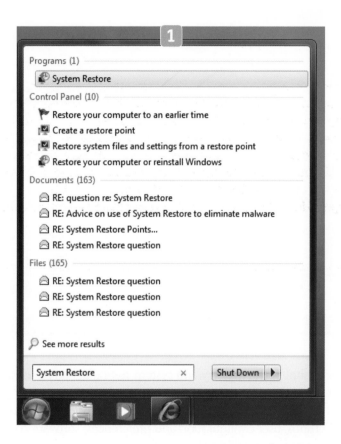

 ALERT: System Restore can't be enabled unless the computer has at least 300 MB of free space on the hard disk, or if the disk is smaller than 1 GB.

 DID YOU KNOW?
Because System Restore works only with its own system files, running System Restore will not affect any of your personal data. Your pictures, email, documents, music, etc. will not be deleted or changed.

2 Click Next to accept and apply the recommended restore point.

3 Click Finish.

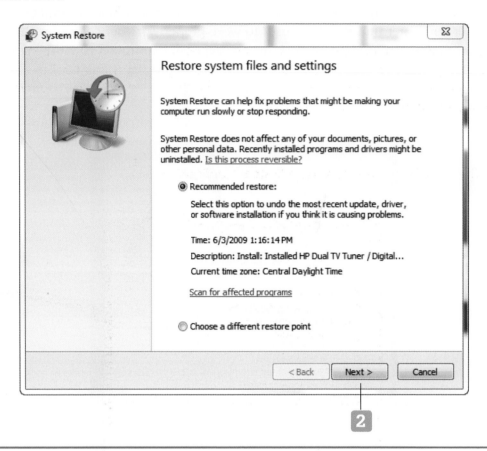

2

WHAT DOES THIS MEAN?

Restore point: a snapshot of the Registry and system state that can be used to make an unstable computer stable again.

Registry: a part of the operating system that contains information about hardware configuration and settings, user configuration and preferences, software configuration and preferences, and other system-specific information.

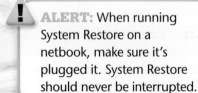 **ALERT:** When running System Restore on a netbook, make sure it's plugged it. System Restore should never be interrupted.

HOT TIP: Many problems occur due to loose or disconnected cables. A mouse can't work unless it's plugged in or its wireless component is. A cable modem can't work unless it's connected securely to the computer and the wall. When troubleshooting, always check your connections.

Disable unwanted start-up items

Lots of programs and applications start when you boot your computer. This causes the start-up process to take longer than it should, and programs that start also run in the background, slowing down computer performance. You should disable unwanted start-up items to improve all-round performance.

1 Click Start.

2 In the Start Search window, type System Configuration.

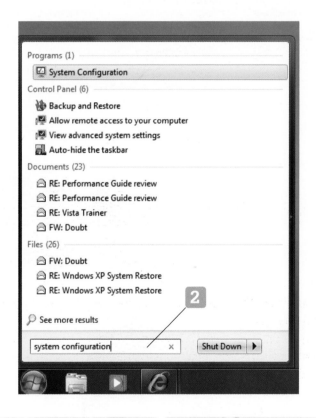

? DID YOU KNOW?
Even if you disable a program from starting when Windows does, you can start it when you need it by clicking it in the Start and All Programs menu.

! ALERT: Do not deselect anything you don't recognise or the operating system!

3 Under Programs, click System Configuration.

4 From the Startup tab, deselect third-party programs you recognise but do not use daily.

5 Click OK.

HOT TIP: If you see a long list under the System Configuration's Startup tab, go through it carefully and consider uninstalling unwanted programs from Control Panel.

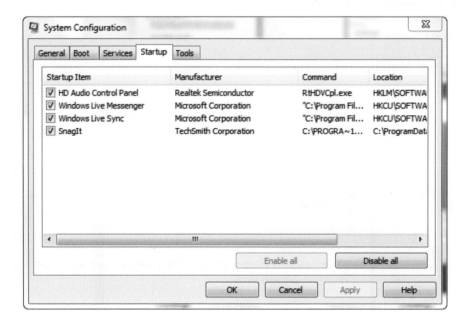

ALERT: You'll have to restart the computer to apply the changes.

Resolve Internet connectivity problems

When you have a problem connecting to your local network or to the Internet, you can often resolve the problem in the Network and Sharing Center.

1 Open the Network and Sharing Center.

2 Click the red X.

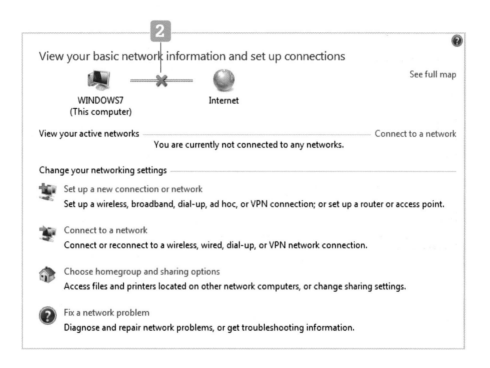

ALERT: Make sure your cable modem, router, cables, and other hardware are properly connected, plugged in and turned on.

ALERT: You won't see a red X if the network is functioning properly.

? DID YOU KNOW? Almost all of the time, performing the first step will resolve your network problem.

3 Perform the steps in the order they are presented.

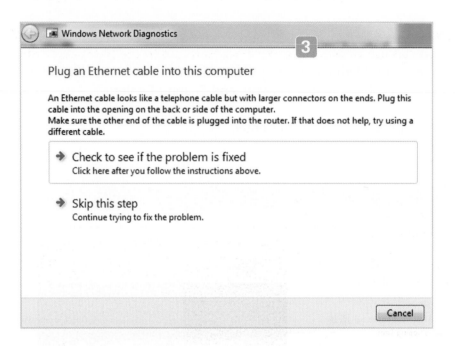

> **⚠ ALERT:** You can't connect your netbook to a wireless network if your wireless features are not enabled.

> **⚠ ALERT:** If prompted to 'reset' your broadband or satellite connection, turn off all hardware including the computer and restart them in the following order: cable/satellite/DSL modem, router, computers.

> **⚠ ALERT:** When restarting a cable or satellite modem, remove any batteries to completely turn off the modem.

Use Device Driver Rollback

If you download and install a new driver for a piece of hardware and it doesn't work properly, you can use Device Driver Rollback to return to the previously installed driver.

1   Click Start.

2   Right-click Computer.

3   Click Properties.

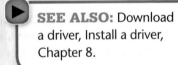

ALERT: You can only rollback to the previous driver. This means that if you have a driver (D), and then install a new driver (D1) and it doesn't work, and then you install another driver (D2) and it doesn't work, using Device Driver Rollback will revert to D1, not the driver (D) before it.

SEE ALSO: Download a driver, Install a driver, Chapter 8.

4 Under Tasks, click Device Manager (not shown).

5 Click the + sign next to the hardware that uses the driver to rollback. It will change to a minus sign.

6 Double-click the device name.

7 Click the Driver tab and click Roll Back Driver.

8 Click OK.

View available hard drive space

Problems can occur when hard drive space gets too low. This can become a problem when you use a computer to record television shows or movies (these require a lot of hard drive space), or if your hard drive is partitioned.

ALERT: If you find you are low on disk space, you'll have to delete unnecessary files and/or applications.

ALERT: If the drive is more than 85 per cent full, delete or move some of the data on it, if possible.

1 Click Start.

2 Click Computer.

3 In the Computer window, right-click the C: drive and choose Properties.

4 View the available space.

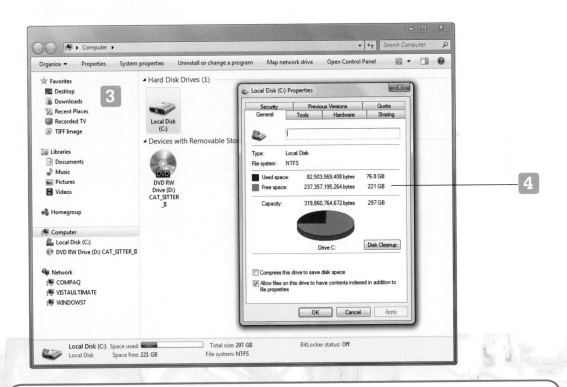

WHAT DOES THIS MEAN?

Partition: some hard drives are configured to have multiple sections, called partitions. The C: partition may have 20 GB available, while the D: partition may have 60. If you save everything to the C: partition (failing to use the D: partition), it can get full quickly.

Delete unnecessary Media Center media

One of the places you'll find data that hogs disk space is in Media Center's storage areas. This is especially true if you record television programmes or movies, or create your own movies. TV and movies take up a lot of hard drive space.

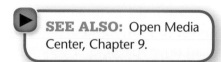
SEE ALSO: Open Media Center, Chapter 9.

1 Open Media Center.

2 Under TV, click Recorded TV.

3 Right-click any recording and click Delete.

4 Repeat as necessary.

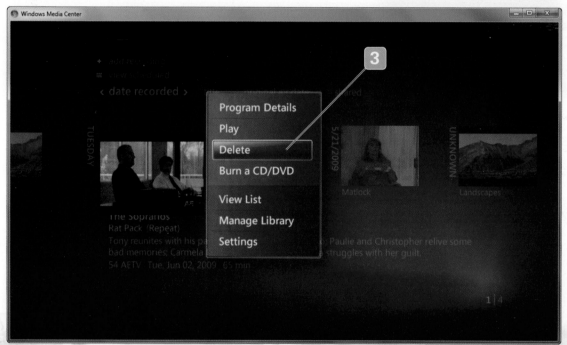

 DID YOU KNOW?
You can also find unwanted media in the Video and Pictures libraries.

HOT TIP: If you see that a series is recording that you don't watch, right-click, choose Series Info, and click Cancel Series.

Uninstall unwanted programs

If you haven't used an application in more than a year, you probably never will. You can uninstall unwanted programs from Control Panel.

1 Click Start, click Control Panel.

2 In Control Panel, click Uninstall a program.

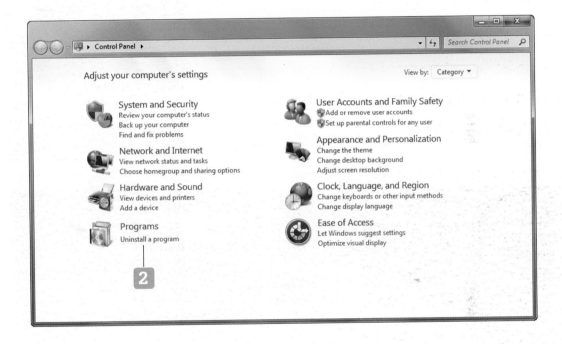

⚠️ **ALERT:** Your netbook may have come with programs you don't even know about. Perform these steps to find out.

🔥 **HOT TIP:** Look for programs in the list that start with the name of the manufacturer of your netbook (Acer, Hewlett-Packard, Dell, etc.).

3 Scroll through the list. Click a program name if you want to uninstall it.

4 Click Uninstall.

5 Follow the prompts to uninstall the program.

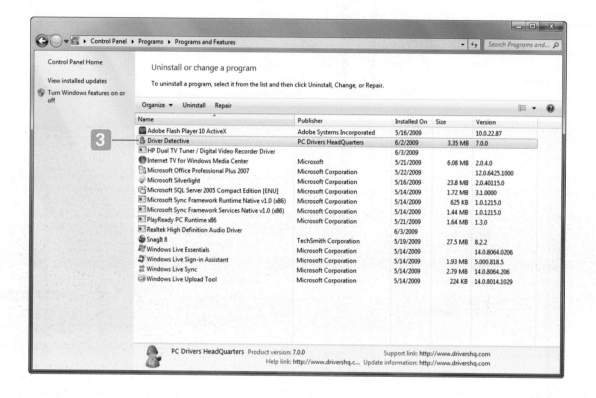

15 Do more with Windows 7

Introduction

There are many features included in Windows 7 that can help you do more, work better, and be more efficient. You have learned about much of this already, and can now create user accounts, scan with Windows Defender, connect to Wi-Fi hotspots, and incorporate Windows Live applications for email and photo editing. There's so much more you can do though.

In this final chapter you'll learn about new features and enhancements as well as how to personalise Windows 7 to suit your tastes and needs. You'll be delighted to see new backgrounds and the option to rotate backgrounds automatically and on a schedule, for instance. You'll enjoy easy access to windows from the taskbar, and the ability to pin applications there for easy access. If you have other Windows 7 computers on your network, you should consider creating a Homegroup for easier sharing. You'll also like the fact that you can 'shake' any window to minimise all of the others. Hang on tight, there's lots to explore!

Learn what's new in Windows 7

Click the Start menu to see the Getting Started option. Hover the mouse over Getting Started to see the pop-out menu. There are several options including, but not limited to, Discover Windows 7, Personalize Windows, Transfer your files, Share with a homegroup and Back up your files, among others.

1 Click Start, then click Getting Started. (When you click Getting Started the Getting Started window opens.)

2 Double-click Go online to find out what's new in Windows 7. You'll have to be connected to the Internet to go online and find out what's new. If you're not online yet, come back to this when you are.

3 Click Tour Windows 7, or browse through the pages to see what's new.

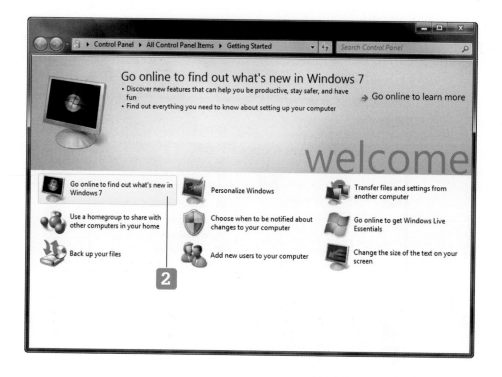

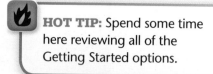 **HOT TIP:** Spend some time here reviewing all of the Getting Started options.

Change the desktop background

If you have yet to personalise the picture on the desktop, now's the time to do that. That picture is called the background.

1 Right-click an empty area of the desktop.

2 Click Personalize.

3 Click Desktop Background.

4 For Location, select Windows Desktop Backgrounds. If it is not chosen already, click the down arrow to locate it.

5 Use the scroll bars to locate the wallpaper to use as your desktop background.

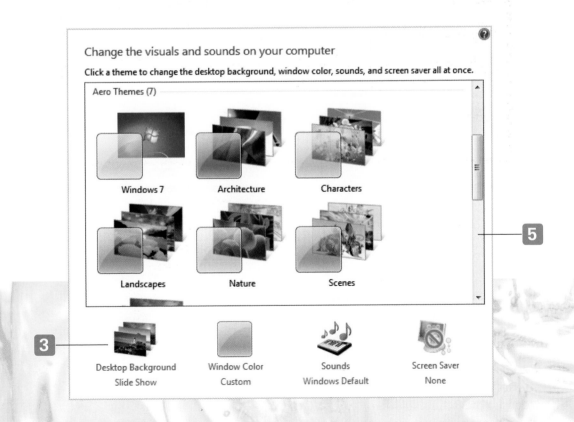

6 Select a background to use or select multiple backgrounds as shown here.

7 Select a positioning option (the default, Fill, is the most common).

8 Change how often to change the backgrounds, if you selected more than one.

9 Click Save changes.

10 Click the red X in the top right corner of the Personalization window to close it.

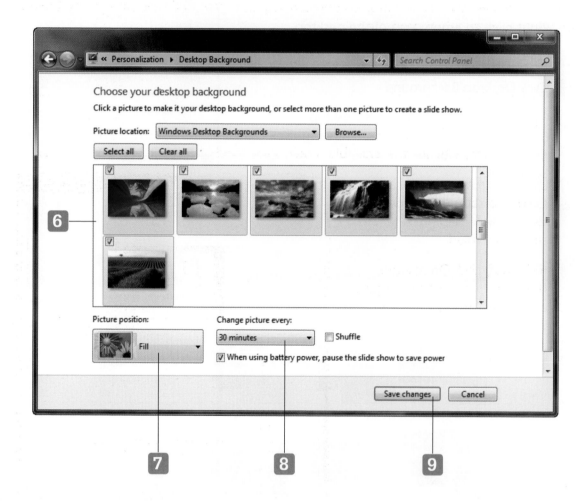

? DID YOU KNOW?

You can click the Browse button to locate a picture you've taken, acquired, or otherwise saved to your netbook, and use it for a desktop background. Pictures are usually found in the Pictures folder.

Change the screen saver

A screen saver is a picture or animation that covers your screen and appears after your computer has been idle for a specific amount of time that you set. Screen savers are used either for visual enhancement or as a security feature. For security, you can configure your screen saver to require a password on waking up, which happens when you move the mouse or hit a key on the keyboard. Requiring a password means that once the screen saver is running, no one can log onto your netbook but you, by typing in your password when prompted.

1 Right-click an empty area of the desktop.

2 Click Personalize.

3 Click Screen Saver.

4 Click the arrow to see the available screen savers and select one.

5 Use the arrows to change how long to wait before the screen saver is enabled.

6 If desired, click On resume, display logon screen to require a password to log back into the netbook.

7 Click OK.

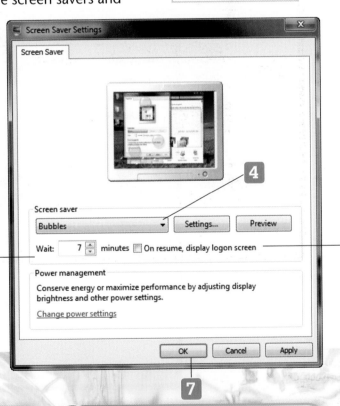

? DID YOU KNOW?

It used to be that screen savers 'saved' your computer screen from image burn-in, but that is no longer the case.

? DID YOU KNOW?

Select Photos and your screen saver will be a slide show of photos stored in your Pictures folder.

Add desktop icons

When Windows 7 started the first time, it may have had only one item on the desktop, the Recycle Bin. Alternatively, it may have had 20 or more. What appears on your desktop the first time Windows boots up depends on a number of factors, including who manufactured your netbook.

1 Right-click an empty area of the desktop.

2 Click Personalize.

3 Click Change desktop icons.

4 Select the desktop icons you want to appear on your desktop.

5 Click OK.

Control Panel Home

Change desktop icons ── **3**
Change mouse pointers
Change your account picture

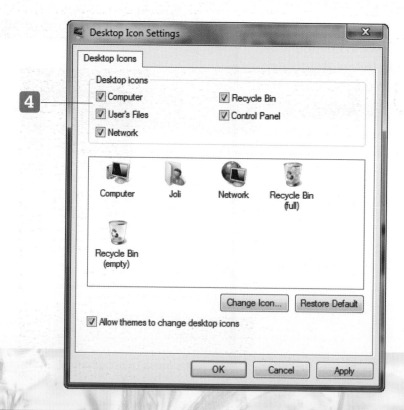

WHAT DOES THIS MEAN?
Icon: a visual representation of an application, feature, or program.

HOT TIP: You can remove desktop icons by deselecting them here.

Create a shortcut on the desktop for a program or application

Shortcuts you place on the desktop let you access folders, files, programs and other items by double-clicking them. Shortcuts always appear with an arrow beside them (or on them, actually). The easiest way to create a shortcut to a program (or other item) you access often is to locate it and right-click it. To create a shortcut for a program installed on your netbook, you'll have to find it in the All Programs menu, as detailed here.

1 Click Start, and then click All Programs.

2 Locate the program you'd like to create a shortcut for and right-click it.

3 Click Send to.

4 Click Desktop (create shortcut).

 HOT TIP: You can create a shortcut for a file, folder, picture, song, or other item by locating it and right-clicking, as detailed in this section.

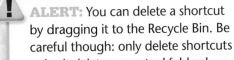 **ALERT:** You can delete a shortcut by dragging it to the Recycle Bin. Be careful though: only delete shortcuts – don't delete any actual folders!

Search for anything from the Start menu

To locate a program, file, folder, song, picture or anything else stored on your netbook, type a little about it in the Start Search window. Just type in what you're looking for and select the appropriate item from the list. Note that when you search using the Start Search window, all kinds of results will appear, including email, applications, documents and pictures.

1 Click Start.

2 In the Start Search window, type Media.

3 Note the results.

4 Click any result to open it. If you want to open Windows Media Player, click it once. Note that it's under Programs.

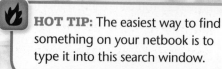

HOT TIP: The easiest way to find something on your netbook is to type it into this search window.

Add a gadget to the desktop

Gadgets sit on your desktop and offer information about the weather, time and date, as well as access to your contacts, productivity tools, and CPU usage. You can even have a slide show of your favourite pictures. You can customise your desktop by adding gadgets and customising them to meet your needs.

1 In the Start Search window, type Gadgets.

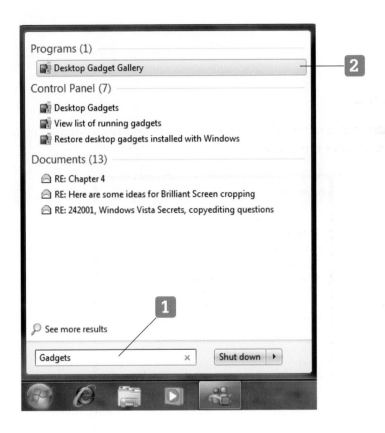

2 Under Programs select Desktop Gadget Gallery.

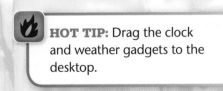 **HOT TIP:** Drag the clock and weather gadgets to the desktop.

ALERT: You won't get up-to-date information on the weather, stocks and other real-time gadgets unless you're connected to the Internet.

3 Drag any gadget to the desktop. You can drag as many as you like.

4 Click the X in the top right corner of the Desktop Gadget Gallery to close it.

ALERT: The Stocks gadget runs about 15 minutes behind real-time stock data, so don't start buying and selling based on what you see here!

Set the time on the clock gadget

Almost all gadgets offer a wrench icon when you position your mouse over them. You can use this icon to access settings for the gadget. The first thing you may want to set is the time on the clock gadget.

1 Position the mouse pointer over the clock you dragged to the desktop. Look for the small x and the wrench to appear. Note that clicking the x will remove the gadget from the desktop. Clicking the wrench will open the gadget's properties, if properties are available.

2 Click the arrow in the Time zone window and select your time zone from the list.

3 Click the right arrow underneath the clock to change the clock type. Type a clock name if you like.

4 Click the left and right arrows to select a new clock, if desired.

5 Click OK.

Configure the taskbar

The taskbar has a new look. It is transparent and blends in nicely with desktop. You can still configure the taskbar by right-clicking and choosing Properties, and you can still lock or hide the taskbar using the options on the Properties page. You can also enable a new feature called Aero Peek.

1 Right-click the taskbar and click Properties.

2 Make changes as desired. Leave Aero Peek enabled.

3 Click OK.

DID YOU KNOW?
You can click Lock the taskbar to keep the taskbar from being accidentally moved or edited.

? DID YOU KNOW?
Aero Peek allows you to preview the Desktop without minimising your windows. To try this out, position your mouse over the farthest right part of the Taskbar to show the Desktop.

HOT TIP: Click the Start Menu and Toolbars tabs to make changes as desired.

HOT TIP: Hide the taskbar for more screen 'real estate'.

Pin icons to the taskbar

If there's a program you use often, consider pinning it to the taskbar. That way, you can access it with a single click of the mouse.

1 Locate the program you want to pin to the taskbar in the Start menu (or the All Programs menu).

2 Right-click it and choose Pin to Taskbar.

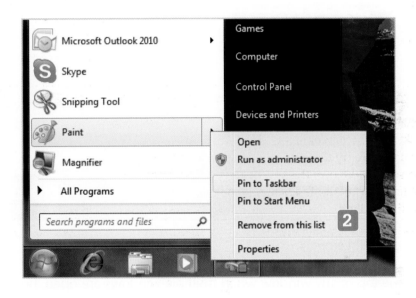

DID YOU KNOW?

From this same area you can pin an icon to the Start menu or remove an item from the Start Menu or All Programs list.

Use Shake, Jump Lists, Snap and Peek

Often you'll work with multiple windows open at once. You need ways to manipulate and move those windows around quickly. There are lots of desktop enhancements to help you with this. First, open four or five windows, as shown here.

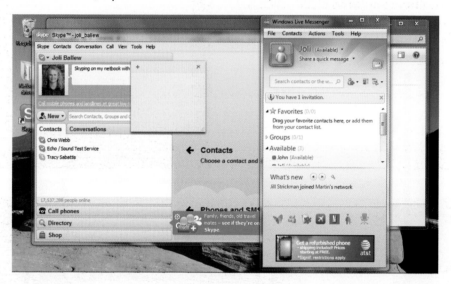

Now, try these enhancements:

1 Left-click the top of any window when multiple windows are open, hold down the mouse key and 'shake' the window back and forth. All open windows except that one will be minimised to the taskbar. Repeat to restore the minimised windows.

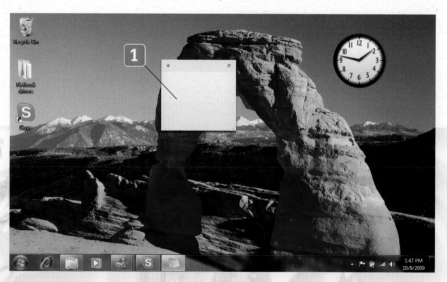

2 Right-click any item on the taskbar to view its 'jump list'.

3 Drag any open window off the left or right side of the desktop to have it automatically resized to take up half the screen. It 'snaps' into place.

4 With multiple windows open, click the Show Desktop option at the far right of the taskbar. You can 'peek' at what's on the desktop.

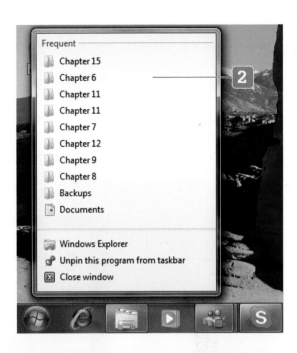

? DID YOU KNOW?

Drag any window upwards to maximise it; drag any maximised window downwards to put it in Restore mode.

Create a homegroup

A homegroup is a new feature that enables Windows 7 computers on a network to more easily share data, pictures, media and documents. You have to create a homegroup on a Windows 7 computer, and other Windows 7 PCs have to join.

1 Click the Network icon in the taskbar's Notification area.

2 Click Open Network and Sharing Center.

3 Under View your active networks, locate Homegroup.

4 Click Ready to Create. (If you see Ready to Join, a homegroup has already been created on another Windows 7 PC on the network.)

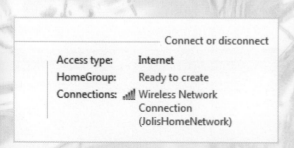

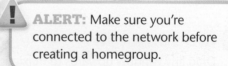
ALERT: Make sure you're connected to the network before creating a homegroup.

5 Click Create a homegroup.

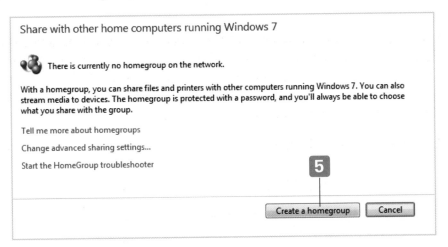

6 Select the items to share. By default, Pictures, Music, Printers and Videos are selected and Documents are not. Click Next.

7 Write down the password and click Finish (not shown).

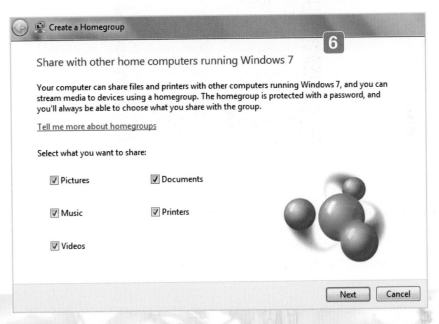

? **DID YOU KNOW?**

You can view the homegroup password from Control Panel, Network and Internet, Homegroup if you forget it. You can also change the password here.

Join a homegroup

Once a homegroup has been created on any Windows 7 computer connected to the home network, other Windows 7 PCs can join.

1 Click the Network icon in the taskbar's Notification area.

2 Click Open Network and Sharing Center.

3 Under View your active networks, locate HomeGroup.

4 Click Available to join.

5 Click Join now and then select the items you want to share (not shown). Click Next.

6 Type the homegroup password and click Next. Click Finish. Note that when you connect a new Windows 7 PC to your network, you'll be prompted to join the homegroup during the set-up process.

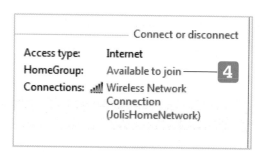

```
                                        Connect or disconnect
Access type:     Internet
HomeGroup:       Available to join ──── 4
Connections: .ıll Wireless Network
                  Connection
                  (JolisHomeNetwork)
```

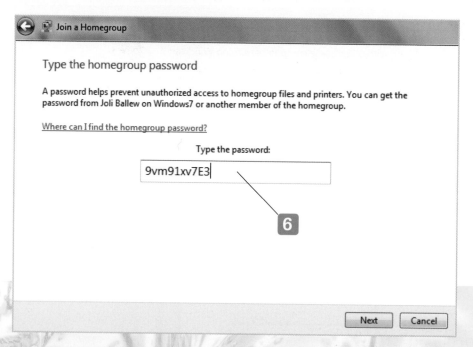

Join a Homegroup

Type the homegroup password

A password helps prevent unauthorized access to homegroup files and printers. You can get the password from Joli Ballew on Windows7 or another member of the homegroup.

Where can I find the homegroup password?

Type the password:

9vm91xv7E3

6

Next   Cancel

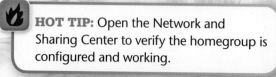

HOT TIP: Open the Network and Sharing Center to verify the homegroup is configured and working.

Explore libraries

Libraries are new to Windows 7. You still save documents to the Documents folder and pictures to the Pictures folder, but Windows 7 keeps an eye on what you're saving and assigns the data to one of several categories. The libraries hold the data related to those categories.

1 Click Start.

2 Click your user name.

3 Note the available libraries: Documents, Music, Pictures and Videos.

4 Double-click any library to see what's inside.

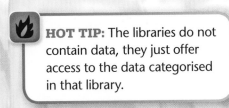 **HOT TIP:** The libraries do not contain data, they just offer access to the data categorised in that library.

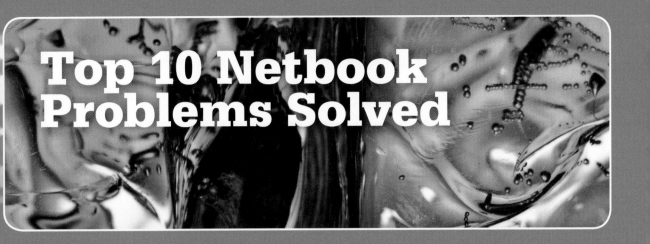

Top 10 Netbook Problems Solved

Problem 1: I'm within range of a public or private wireless network, but I can't see it and I can't log in.

Before you can connect to a Wi-Fi network, the Wi-Fi feature on your netbook must be enabled. Some netbooks have a switch on the outside of the netbook, while others have a key combination on the keyboard. You should refer to your user's manual to find out exactly how to enable and disable Wi-Fi in this manner.

If you can't find the switch or key combination to enable Wi-Fi, you can enable and disable Wi-Fi from the Mobility Center.

1 Click Start, and in the Start Search box type Mobility.

ALERT: When wireless is enabled, Windows 7 constantly searches for wireless signals, which uses battery power. You may have turned off Wi-Fi for this reason.

2 Click Mobility Center.

3 Click Turn wireless off to disable Wi-Fi.

4 Click Turn wireless on to enable it.

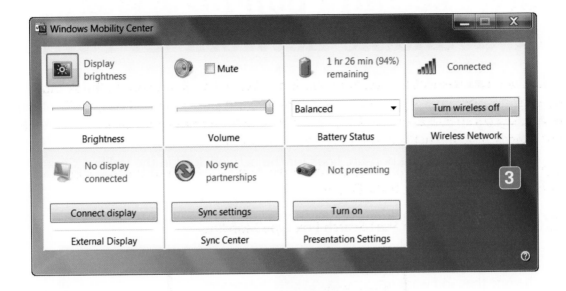

Problem 2: I'm in a coffee shop that offers free Wi-Fi, but I didn't see any pop-up about the available network (or I was unable to click the pop-up in time). How can I join now?

It's okay if you missed the pop-up. Look for the network icon in the taskbar. Click it to see the available wireless networks.

1 Click the network icon in the Notification area.

2 If more than one wireless network is available, locate the one that you want to use and click Connect.

ALERT: You will probably want to choose the wireless network with the most green bars.

3 When prompted, choose Public network.

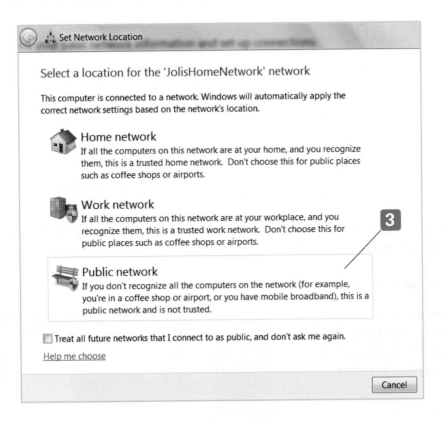

Set Network Location

Select a location for the 'JolisHomeNetwork' network

This computer is connected to a network. Windows will automatically apply the correct network settings based on the network's location.

Home network
If all the computers on this network are at your home, and you recognize them, this is a trusted home network. Don't choose this for public places such as coffee shops or airports.

Work network
If all the computers on this network are at your workplace, and you recognize them, this is a trusted work network. Don't choose this for public places such as coffee shops or airports.

3

Public network
If you don't recognize all the computers on the network (for example, you're in a coffee shop or airport, or you have mobile broadband), this is a public network and is not trusted.

☐ Treat all future networks that I connect to as public, and don't ask me again.

Help me choose

Cancel

ALERT: Wi-Fi must be enabled in the Mobility Center or via a switch or keyboard combination to connect to a Wi-Fi network.

Problem 3: I've downloaded and installed Windows Live Messenger, I have contacts, and my webcam is working. I still can't initiate a video conversation. What's up?

You need to run the Audio and Tuning Wizard to set up your webcam to work with Windows Live Messenger. You'll also need to configure your microphone and speakers. Don't worry, a wizard will walk you through it.

1 Open Windows Live Messenger and log in.

2 Click Tools, and click Audio and video setup.

HOT TIP: If you can't see the Tools menu shown here, click the Alt key on your keyboard.

3 Click Test to test your speakers, and then speak into the microphone to verify it is working properly. Click Next.

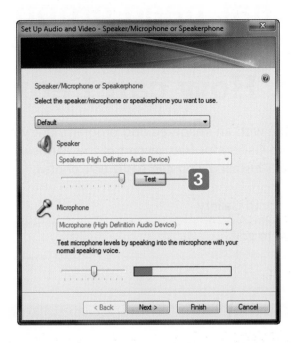

4 Select your webcam from the list. You should see yourself in it.

5 Click Webcam Settings to configure additional options.

6 Click OK and Finish.

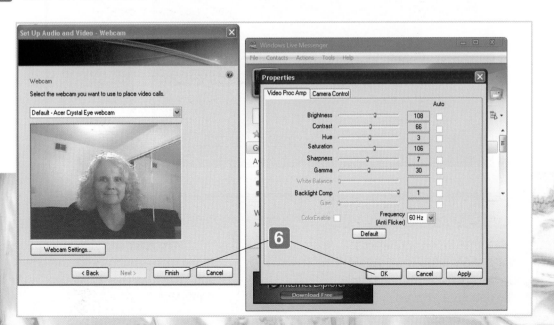

Problem 4: I have several pictures that need cropping, are too dark, too light or have other problems. How can I edit them?

Windows 7 does not come with an image-editing program, but you can download and install Windows Live Photo Gallery for free, as part of the Windows Live Essentials suite of applications. Once that's installed, you can easily edit photos.

1 Open Windows Live Photo Gallery.

2 Double-click a picture to edit.

3 Click Fix.

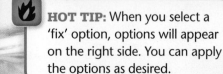 **HOT TIP:** When you select a 'fix' option, options will appear on the right side. You can apply the options as desired.

ALERT: After applying any option, to see more options, click the down and up arrows that will appear in the right pane.

4 Click Auto adjust to fix problems with the photo. Adjustments will be made automatically.

5 Continue adjusting as desired, using the sliders to adjust the settings.

6 Click Crop photo.

7 Configure as desired, dragging the crop box around the image and resizing it as needed.

8 Click Apply.

HOT TIP: Click the Back to Gallery button and your changes will be saved automatically.

Problem 5: Where is Outlook Express or Windows Mail? Where's my email?

Windows 7 does not come with an email program. You have to download one. In this book, we have used Windows Live Mail, part of the Windows Live Essentials suite of application. Once downloaded, you can configure your email addresses.

1 Open Internet Explorer and go to http://download.live.com/.

2 Look for the Download button and click it. You'll be prompted to click Download once more on the next screen.

3 Click Run, and when prompted, click Yes.

4 When prompted, select the items to download. You can select all of the items or only some of them. (Make sure to at least select Live Mail, Live Messenger and Live Photo Gallery.)

5 Click Install.

6 When prompted to select your settings, make the desired choices. You can't go wrong here; there are no bad options.

Download **2**

System requirements

Programs you can download include:

Messenger
Mail
Writer
Photo Gallery
Movie Maker
Family Safety
Toolbar

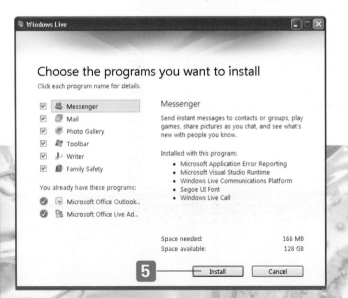

? DID YOU KNOW?
Now you'll need to configure Windows Live Mail with your email addresses and passwords.

Problem 6: I installed a driver or program and now my computer isn't behaving the way it should.

System Restore regularly creates and saves *restore points* that contain information about your computer that Windows uses to work properly. If your computer starts acting funny, you can use System Restore to restore your computer to a time when the computer was working properly.

1 Open System Restore.

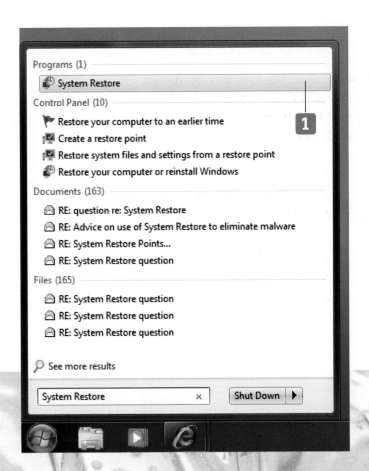

2 Click Next to accept and apply the recommended restore point.

3 Click Finish.

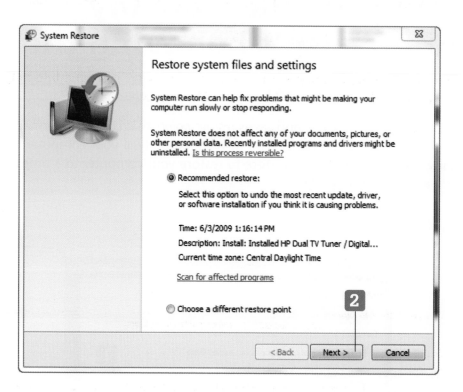

Problem 7: I was connected to the Internet and/or my local network and now I'm not.

When you have a problem connecting to your local network or to the Internet, you can often resolve the problem in the Network and Sharing Center.

1 Open the Network and Sharing Center.

2 Click the red X.

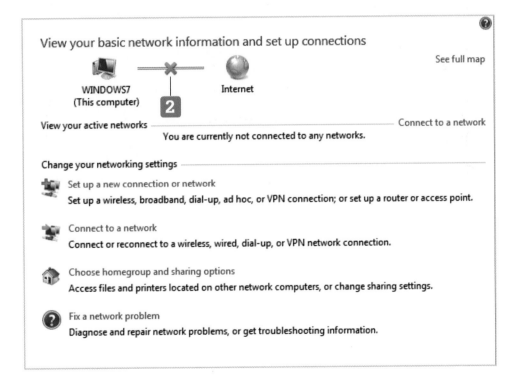

? DID YOU KNOW?
Almost all of the time, performing the first step will resolve your network problem.

3 Perform the steps in the order they are presented.

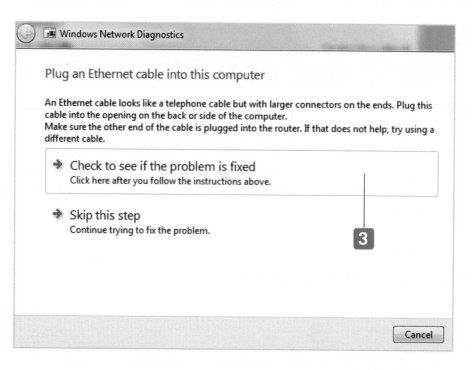

Problem 8: My new netbook came with a lot of programs I'll never use and I want them gone!

Most manufacturers add their own 'touches' to the netbooks they manufacture. You probably won't need many of them. Additionally, you may have programs you haven't used in a while and know you'll never use again. You can uninstall unwanted programs from Control Panel.

1 Click Start, click Control Panel.

2 In Control Panel, click Uninstall a program.

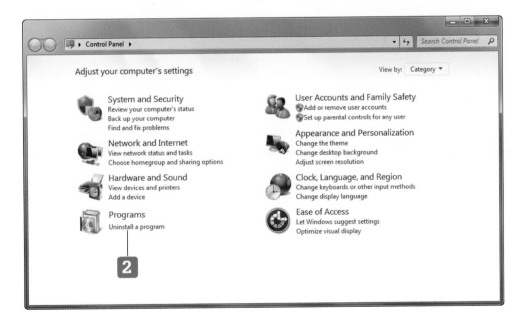

ALERT: Your netbook may have come with programs you don't even know about. Perform these steps to find out.

HOT TIP: Look for programs in the list that start with the name of the manufacturer of your netbook (Acer, Hewlett-Packard, Dell, etc.)

3 Scroll through the list. Click a program name if you want to uninstall it.

4 Click Uninstall.

5 Follow the prompts to uninstall the program.

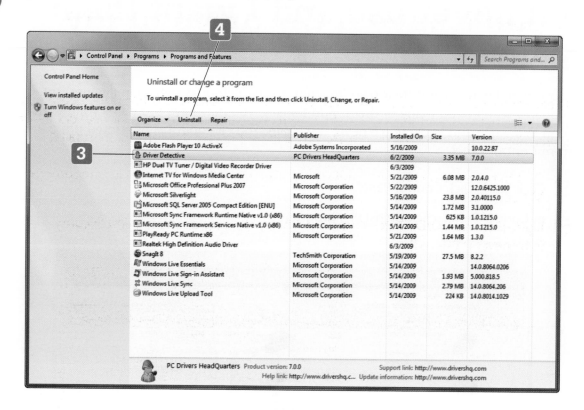

Problem 9: I need to install software that is on a CD, but I don't have a CD drive in my netbook. What can I do?

There are several ways to install software from a CD, and one is to connect the netbook to your home network and share a disk drive from another computer on your network. Once shared, insert the CD and browse to the installation disk over the network to install it.

1 On the networked computer (not your netbook), click Start and click Computer (or My Computer.)

2 Right-click the CD/DVD drive and click Share, Sharing, or Sharing and Security (whichever is offered).

? DID YOU KNOW?

After sharing a drive, you'll see an icon on it that shows it's shared.

3 Locate the option to share the drive. You may have to click Advanced Sharing. The steps depend on what operating and file system the computer uses.

4 Click OK or Apply to save the changes.

5 On your netbook, click the folder icon on the taskbar.

6 Click Network, and click the computer the drive resides on.

7 Double-click to open the shared drive, often D:, E:, or something similar.

8 Locate the installation program and run it.

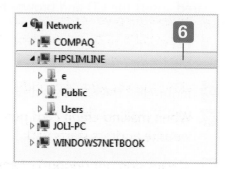

HOT TIP: The installation icon often resembles the program or company logo.

? DID YOU KNOW?
Installation over a network takes longer than installing from a CD or DVD on the same computer.

Problem 10: I'm online a lot and I worry about staying safe. What can I do?

When you're online, make sure to follow these guidelines.

1 If you are connecting to a free Wi-Fi hotspot or a public network, make sure you select Public when prompted by Windows 7.

2 Always keep your netbook secure with anti-virus software. Windows 7 does not come with any, so you'll have to install your own. Consider Microsoft's new Security Essentials; for now, anyway, it's free.

3 Limit the amount of confidential information you store on the Internet.

4 When making credit card purchases or travel reservations, always make sure the website address starts with https://.

5 Always sign out (logout) of any secure website you enter.

6 If you're surfing the Web in a public place, protect yourself when you enter passwords and credit card information. Hide your keystrokes, don't flash your credit card around, and make sure you've selected Public for the network type.

HOT TIP: The s after http lets you know it's a secure site.

? DID YOU KNOW?
When you connect to a network you know, like a network in your home, you select Home (or Work).

! ALERT: Don't put your address and phone number on Facebook or any other social networking sites.

USE YOUR COMPUTER WITH CONFIDENCE

9780273723547

9780273723509

9780273723486

9780273723479

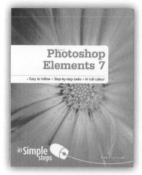

9780273723523

9780273723493

9780273723554

In Simple Steps guides guarantee immediate results. They teach you exactly what you want and need to know on any application; from the most essential tasks to master through to solving the most common problems you'll encounter.

- **<u>Practical</u>** – explains and provides practical solutions to the most commonly encountered problems

- **<u>Easy to understand</u>** – jargon and technical terms explained in simple English

- **<u>Visual</u>** – full colour large screen shots

Practical. Simple. Fast.

in Simple steps